THE COMPLETE GUIDE TO
DIGITAL
3D DESIGN

THE COMPLETE GUIDE TO
DIGITAL
3D DESIGN

Simon Danaher

ILEX

First published in the United Kingdom in 2004 by

I L E X

The Old Candlemakers,
West Street,
Lewes,
East Sussex,
BN7 2NZ
www.ilex-press.com

Copyright © 2004 by The Ilex Press Limited

This book was conceived by
ILEX, Cambridge, England

Publisher: Alastair Campbell
Executive Publisher: Sophie Collins
Creative Director: Peter Bridgewater
Editorial Director: Steve Luck
Editor: Stuart Andrews
Design Manager: Tony Seddon
Designer: Jon Raimes
Artwork Assistant: Joanna Clinch
Development Art Director: Graham Davis
Technical Art Editor: Nicholas Rowland

British Library Cataloguing-in-Publication Data
A catalogue record for this book is available from the
British Library

ISBN 1-904705-38-3

Printed and bound in China

For more on Digital 3D Design visit:
www.cg3duk.web-linked.com

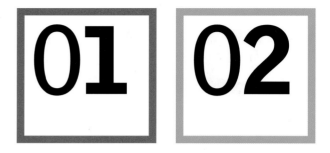

CONTENTS

03 **04** **05** **06** **06**

HISTORY OF 3D

01

Above: **In 1984, Apple's Macintosh computer introduced the first graphical user interface and the whole 'desktop' metaphor, still in use in OS X and Windows XP today.**

PART 01. HISTORY

CHAPTER ONE

3D PAST

IN THE BEGINNING Computers have revolutionized the way we create and work with images and graphics. It's sometimes hard to grasp the vast, fundamental shift that technology has caused in the creation and distribution of visual media, especially since the actual workings of the technology still remain a mystery to many.

From the 7th through the 13th centuries, books – usually religious in nature – were created one by one by hand, and it took a huge amount of dedication to create such beautiful manuscripts. While the Chinese developed a form of simple printing at the beginning of the 11th century, it wasn't until the 15th century, when the German inventor Johannes Gutenberg (c 1390-1468) invented his printing press using movable type, that the production and distribution of printed text and images in volume was possible.

Centuries later, printing was still done mechanically. Great newspaper presses could churn out thousands of copies bearing text and photographic images, and by the mid-19th century they were able to do so in colour. Before any book or newspaper could be printed, however, the production and layout still needed to be done by hand first.

Then came the computer. A novelty at first, computers were created as counting machines and calculators for scientists and mathematicians. Soon simple displays were invented for displaying text and later graphics. Sophisticated interfaces were developed, and in 1984 Apple Computer released the Macintosh sporting its 'desktop' metaphor interface. With the introduction of Aldus Pagemaker and laser printers, the desktop-printing revolution arrived and the rest is history.

The advent of personal computers featuring easy-to-use graphical interfaces was the spark that ignited the desktop-publishing revolution. This marked a huge change, enabling anyone with access to a computer to create and manipulate text and images. However, there were more than a few who were interested in images alone.

With the introduction of the Apple Macintosh and programs like Aldus Pagemaker (later to become Adobe Pagemaker) the role of the computer in publishing was set. With a computer that featured an easy-to-use graphical interface, it was simple to lay out text and images in the digital realm, then transfer them to an image-setter to produce colour separations for printing.

The Postscript language bridged the gap between the computer and the real world, converting digital fonts and graphics into real printed text and graphics. Similarly, digital scanners took photographic prints or negatives and converted them into digital images for manipulation on the computer.

It was a program that could take digital images and make adjustments to them that sparked the digital-imaging revolution. Photoshop was designed by brothers John and Thomas Knoll to assist John in his work at the legendary special-effects company, Industrial Light and Magic (John would later become an important figure in the 3D industry, too). The program allowed simple colour correction and file format conversion, plus basic painting and cloning tools. Suddenly it was possible to do rather impressive things with digital images—things that were previously impossible. The digital darkroom was born.

Photoshop was licenced to Adobe and it has since become the most popular and important imaging program. It is also an incredibly important application for 3D artists, for whom it is used to create textures or composite 3D renders with other images.

The combination of Photoshop and early CAD (Computer Aided Design) software paved the way for new types of digital art. We can now use computers to generate photorealistic images using 3D software. We can combine 3D graphics with 2D photos or movie footage to combine computer-generated imagery with imagery from the real world. We can even take 3D objects designed in the digital realm and reproduce them in the real world through processes such as stereolithography and computer-controlled manufacturing. Increasingly, anything is possible.

Above: **Brothers John and Thomas Knoll developed Photoshop to help John with work he did at Industrial Light and Magic. After some initial difficulty in promoting the product they licenced it to Adobe.**

Left: **Arguably the most important software development in the graphics industry, Photoshop was the first program that could be used to manipulate images in a creative way. It spawned a generation of digital artists.**

EARLY 3D While 2D graphics and desktop publishing were becoming established on the computer, 3D graphics technology was still only available to those in research labs at universities and large companies with powerful computers. Yet the development of 3D graphics could be traced back much further, to the 1960s.

In the early 1960s Charles Csuri, a traditional artist (and talented football player) became interested in the use of computers for creating images. Arguably the first 'digital artist' he pioneered the creative use of computers in art, producing images and even animations as early as 1965. Working with mathematicians, Csuri even developed a way to plot 3D surfaces and recreate them in wood as sculpture.

Ivan Sutherland, working on his doctoral thesis at MIT, produced a program called Sketchpad for the TX-2 computer, then one of the most advanced in the world. He would later devise computer-graphics simulation systems for helicopter pilots, possibly the first 'virtual reality' system ever.

In the 1970s computers became vastly more powerful and smaller. People like Jim Blinn, Martin Newell, Frank Crowe and Ed Catmull at the University of Utah, and Michael Chou at NYIT, harnessed the power of the computer to devise ways to build models or real-world objects in 3D space inside the computer. Technologies that are still used today in computer-graphics programs were developed to 'shade' the surfaces that were built and give them a photographic quality. Many of the advancements they developed are still in use today including shading, depth sorting, texture, environment and bump mapping, and antialiasing techniques.

Left: Ivan Sutherland pioneered a lot of research into digital graphics and did so as early as the 1960s. He now works at Sun Microsystems.

Above: Charles Csuri was probably the first digital artist. In the early 1960s he developed the first computer-generated artworks.

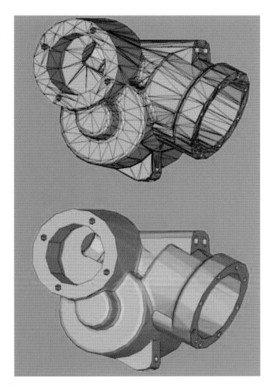

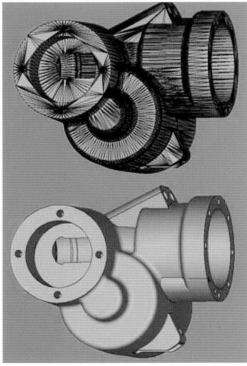

Left: **The standard file format for stereolithography, .STL, stores the object's geometry as a set of triangular facets, which define its outer and/or inner surface. The .STL file can be imported and manipulated in 3D and industrial CAD applications, provided they have the right converters.**

Above: **CAD and Mechanical design applications, such as SolidWorks, go beyond object modeling and animation to component assembly and stress analysis. With CAD and CAM applications, photorealism isn't as vital as clarity, accuracy and the ease and speed of use.**

3D SIMULATION, 3D VIEWING, AND VR
Simulation is another application for 3D graphics, and because it is often generated in real time, it has a lot in common with game production. You can simulate just about anything in 3D so its field of application is very broad. Some of the more common uses for 3D simulators include aviation and aircraft training, medical imaging and, of course, entertainment applications such as theme park rides.

Real-time simulation systems have been used in many situations, from scientific research to games and entertainment. Virtual reality is an offshoot that combines real-time 3D graphics with 3D goggles or some other device to create the impression of a real environment enveloping the user. Many attempts have been made at creating viable virtual-reality systems, but it seems that it has not caught on, at least for most of us. But 3D VR systems still tend to be expensive, and so their application is limited. As a way to interface humans and computers, 3D has not yet been successfully exploited and, although a nice idea, it may be that VR is not the right approach.

3D shutter glasses can be used for viewing videos and DVDs filmed with stereoscopic cameras. These are relatively inexpensive but the film libraries are not that extensive. A stereoscopic camera films the action from two slightly separated lenses (corresponding to the positions of our two eyes). These two images are combined into fields in a single video frame and play concurrently. Televisions display each field alternately at 60hz (60 times a second) and the shutter glasses block each eye at the same frequency using liquid

crystal lenses. In this way, the left eye receives only the left image and the right eye only the right image. This can cause annoying flickering, so a technique called vertical sync doubling is often used, which effectively doubles the rate at which images are displayed, reducing the effect.

Such systems can be used to view 3D-rendered animations that have been stereoscopically rendered. This is not a difficult process to achieve, and in fact any 3D animation package can generate the images required for stereoscopic 3D. It's just the way the two images are combined that enables them to be viewed using shutter glasses. A motion-graphics application such as Adobe After Effects can also be used for this, using the field interlacing options.

3D shutter glasses are also used for viewing 3D games in true 3D. The glasses connect to the video card in the computer, and because computer monitors can usually display at much higher frequencies than a TV set, vertical sync doubling is not usually required.

Left: **Virtual-reality systems attempt to simulate an immersive environment with which the user can interact. Goggle-based VR systems were typically bulky and uncomfortable to use for long periods, but the technology is steadily slimming down.**

Below: **Many 3D accelerator cards enable you to connect LCD shutter glasses for playing 3D games in true 3D. With monitors capable of changing images at rates of 100Hz or more, these systems are quite comfortable to use.**

HAPTIC FEEDBACK

3D is used extensively in medical research and training, but one of the problems with 3D graphics is that you can't interact with them physically. However, engineers have devised a way around that problem using haptic feedback systems. These provide physical simulation that correlates with the visual simulation on screen to form the basis of surgical training devices.

Flight simulators also combine haptic feedback and 3D graphics but on quite a different scale. Trainee military and passenger jet pilots spend hundreds of hours in industrial flight simulators which are exact replicas of the cockpits of commercial and military jet planes. The windows are replaced by computer screens displaying the simulated 3D scenery. The cockpit is mounted in a special hydraulic rig that can move the entire system in all axes to give the impression of real flight – turbulence included.

The converse of the use of haptics in simulation is its use in the 3D creation process itself. At one time 3D modeling was often done by plotting the positions of points on the surfaces of a clay model, particularly for organic objects that were difficult to create in 3D directly. It was easy for model builders to make a maquette or sculpture in clay and then digitize it using a sensor pen attached to a computer by a series of jointed arms. These systems have since fallen out of favour partly due to their expense but also due to new photographic 3D digitizing techniques.

The probe concept can be used instead as part of a haptic control system. Such a system lets 3D artists sculpt models using an arm-pen probe. They then receive feedback through the probe, giving the sensation of sculpting a real object.

Above: A flight simulator combines realistic 3D graphics with real movement used for training jet pilots. These expensive systems utilize powerful computers and mimic the characteristics of commercial and military jet planes.

Right: Phantom is a haptic input device (also known as a force-feedback device) produced by Sensable Technologies. It provides tactile feedback to users of 3D software as they sculpt and manipulate 3D objects.

ARCHITECTURE Architecture is a design discipline that deals directly with 3D forms, so 3D graphics fits perfectly with it both as a design and visualization tool. It has also become a way for architects to explore flights of fancy more dramatically than ever before.

Copyright (c) 2003 Chen Qingfeng(Xiamen,China)

Many architects design on the computer, although they may not enter the 3D modeling stage immediately. Ideas may be sketched and worked up in plan form initally, but it's also possible to work directly with 3D software right from the beginning. It's just a matter of individual preference. However, this is a fairly recent development. Traditionally, 3D models were only created once the design and planning was set, since making changes to a 3D model as complex as an entire building would be time-consuming and costly. Modern 3D architectural software offers more creative freedom than ever before. With fast modeling tools and real-time display rendering, architects are allowed to explore their ideas directly in 3D.

These days the focus is more on efficiency and productivity, with programs making use of referencing, instances and procedural models to help to fill in the details of a building (such as prebuilt windows and doors with customizable parameters that can be dragged and dropped into place).

One program of note is called SketchUp by AtLast software. It is designed to be an architect's 3D sketchbook: a program that has the speed and directness of pencil and paper but the power and flexibility of a 3D program. It features smart cursors that detect angles and intersections as you build in 3D.

Opposite: **Using powerful radiosity rendering techniques, highly accurate lighting simulations can be performed in the computer. These beautiful examples by Chen Qingfeng demonstrate the subtle skill of setting up and rendering impressive lighting simulations in 3D.**

Above right: **Using 3D software, architects can explore many different aspects of their buildings, including materials and lighting.**

Right: **This image shows the masses of detail that would typically go into creating a building in 3D. If there are many repeating structures in a model, they can be created using instances – a feature that may come in useful if the architect needs to be able to alter them later. A small part of the building that is repeated hundreds of times can be changed by editing the master object; all the instances update automatically.**

PART 02. 3D IN THE REAL WORLD

CHAPTER TWO

3D IN THE ARTS

DESIGNING IN 3D FOR 2D It may not be immediately apparent that 3D can be a useful tool for the 2D artist working in print or on the Web. However, non-photorealistic rendering techniques mean that 3D software can work in tandem with illustration and image-editing programs to create great 2D artwork.

A recent trend has been towards the use of abstract 3D forms in digital illustration. By combining vector and Photoshop artwork with complex abstract 3D forms, contemporary illustrators have forged a new direction that merges traditional and cutting-edge techniques. 3D programs have played a crucial role in this modern style, becoming a trusted tool in the creative design toolbox.

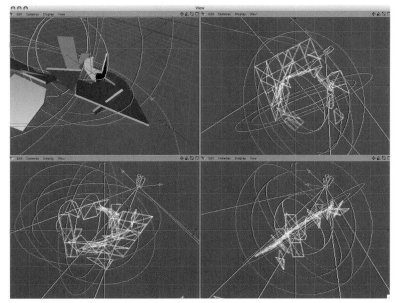

Right: The ability to manipulate perspective in 3D offers a wide range of creative possibilities, too. The computer keeps the perspective correct, even when it is greatly exaggerated.

Below left: 3D can also be used conspicuously for illustration work, but by keeping detail and clutter low and using simple objects and plain surfaces, designers can create cool illustrations that seem half 2D, half 3D.

Below right: Again by avoiding photorealistic pitfalls, designers make 3D applications ideal tools for clean-cut illustration work. Even when using techniques like raytraced reflections, unnatural shapes and structure can prevent images losing that abstract quality.

Above: **A typical low-polygon game character. Note that most of the detail comes from the texture map applied to the model. The model is 'light', geometrically speaking, so it can be rendered interactively.**

Right: **Game developers need to keep polygon counts to a minimum in order to keep the graphics flowing. A 3D tree can be made using two mutually perpendicular triangular polygons. Mapping a tree texture onto each gives a fair impression of a 3D tree that can be viewed from most angles. This is the colour texture.**

Far right: **And this is the alpha channel used to stencil out the tree image from its background.**

part 02. 3D in the real world

3D GAME DESIGN Computer gaming has become a significant part of modern culture, and it's an area in which 3D rules supreme. Early computer games date back almost as far as the computer itself, but it wasn't until the introduction of colour graphics that games really began to enthrall kids and adults. When the first 3D games appeared they were really revolutionary, while the games of today are nothing short of astounding.

3D game production is an involved process. It's quite unlike any of the other creative uses for 3D graphics because of the simple fact that game graphics are generated in real-time. In movie and video production, illustration, or visualization, the final rendered image is produced slowly, because the rendered image needs to be high quality and that takes time. For 3D games the definition of 'quality' is different entirely. It's all about the playability of the game and the speed of the graphics rather than photorealism and in order to achieve this, compromises have to be made elsewhere.

One compromise is to make 3D models with a lower polygon count. That means that the geometry used to create the game scenery and characters is as simple as possible while still having enough detail to be visually interesting. Texture maps are used to make up for the lack of detail in a game model, and this explains the typically 'blocky' look of game characters.

All the 3D graphics you see on screen while you are playing a game will be rendered interactively, at rates of 30 frames a second or more, yet a typical high-resolution frame for a feature film might take three minutes to render. That's a mere 0.056 frames per second. 3D game graphics need to be generated 540 times faster on average than film and broadcast graphics, which puts things into perspective.

While games developers can make use of hardware acceleration and special rendering software such as OpenGL or Direct X, they still need to be efficient in the use of geometry, textures and lighting in order to achieve fast frame rates. Developers often use clever tricks and sleight of hand in order to imply detail that is not actually there. However, as computer hardware has become more powerful, games are becoming richer and more detailed. The current crop of 3D games are incredibly so, featuring real-time reflection maps, detailed models, volumetric effects and more.

Below: **When applied to the two polygons you get a fairly decent-looking tree.**

SPECIAL EFFECTS Arguably the most demanding, visible and visually impressive use of 3D graphics is in effects for film. The applications in this field cover just about every possible use for the technology. In fact movie special-effect production is one of the most potent driving forces in the development of 3D applications. Such vital advances as realistic simulated hair, fur and cloth have all been developed primarily because film production demands them.

Left: **One area that 3D has yet to conquer is that of the digital actor – the 'Synthespian'. While 3D animated creatures, monsters, or cartoon characters have been accepted, it's more difficult to create realistic humans, with all their foibles, complex emotion, and behaviour. The best attempt so far was made by Columbia Pictures and Square Pictures Inc. with the cutting-edge, all-3D film** *Final Fantasy: The Spirits Within* (2001).

Below left: **Desktop 3D applications make it possible for independent artists to create animated movies. Chris Bailey's short** *Major Damage* **was created by a core team of three with assistance from 3D artists worldwide.** Major Damage TM © Copyright 2001 Chris Bailey. All rights reserved.

3D graphics are used to create digital landscapes, seascapes, and scenery, to modify or remove existing buildings, or even recreate ancient ones. 3D graphics are also commonly used to create explosions, laser bolts, digital planets and space scenes, and such effects are now within the budget of even modest movie and TV productions. There are hundreds of 3D studios around the world working on countless movies, and the 3D production industry is set to get even more prolific.

As well as the effects you see on screen, 3D is used as a pre-production tool, too. 3D animated storyboards, known as animatics, are common on big Hollywood productions, and these can be used to work out camera angles and ascertain any difficulties that might occur when shooting real footage that is to be combined with 3D imagery.

Below: Merging live-action footage and 3D graphics seamlessly is essential for creating today's blockbuster special effects. It's rare for an entire shot to be 100 per cent 3D, even in the most intense battle scene. The best 3D work on the big screen, as in *The Lord of the Rings: Return of the King*, comes when live action is combined with digital effects, but the process isn't simple. Matching the lighting, the look and the tone of the movie, plus the movement of the camera, requires the skills of large numbers of talented 3D artists.

DYNAMICS
3D programs have come into their own in the field of producing effects and digital trickery for TV broadcast and movie productions. One area in which 3D programs have improved in recent years is dynamics simulation.

By integrating physical laws and behaviour in 3D programs, developers have enabled 3D artists to create animations that include realistic natural motion. Objects fall as they should under the influence of gravity, rigid bodies collide, shatter and scatter as they should in real life and soft bodies deform as they should during movement.

In 3D, animation is usually done by setting keyframes for various parameters on an object – its position, rotation or colour and so on. For large scenes involving characters or machines with many moving parts, even a simple animation can be a complex business. If you want to throw your character down a flight of stairs, or cause two speeding vehicles to crash, animating by hand is going to be a laborious and painstaking process.

Using dynamics algorithms you let the computer take over and calculate the effects of collisions, gravity and other physical forces for you. These rigid-body simulations can be calculated and converted to keyframes (in a process known as 'baking') so that the calculation only needs to be done once. Like rendering, a physical simulation can require some time to be processed, so converting to keyframes lets the simulation be played back in real time. Having the simulation baked also means it can be edited if necessary using the 3D program's keyframe-editing tool set.

A good example of rigid-body dynamics can be seen in the pod-racing scene from *Star Wars Episode I: The Phantom Menace* (1999). In this scene Maya was used to crash several highly detailed pod-racer models, and to calculate the vast number of parts that

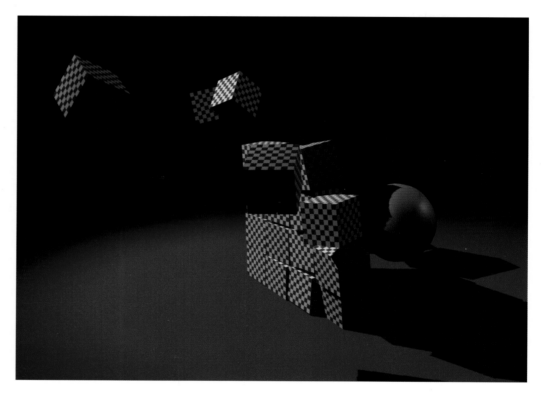

Above: **Using rigid body dynamics, you can set up a collision and let the software calculate the myriad interactions that occur as a result. Such an animation would be next to impossible to create any other way.**

broke off and flew from the tumbling pod-racer engines. The great results speak volumes for the use of dynamics simulation in effects work.

Softbody dynamics is a separate branch of dynamics simulation in which forces and collisions cause the surface of objects to deform. Softbody simulation can be used to animate objects and surfaces that were tricky to do properly before, including water dynamics, cloth and fabric, rubber and the motion of the human body. For the latter, softbody simulation provides a way to add 'jiggle' and bounce at a stroke. This secondary motion (motion that occurs in reaction to the primary movement and which may continue after it has stopped) is essential for the creation of believable characters, especially if they are large, bulky and carry a lot of excess flesh.

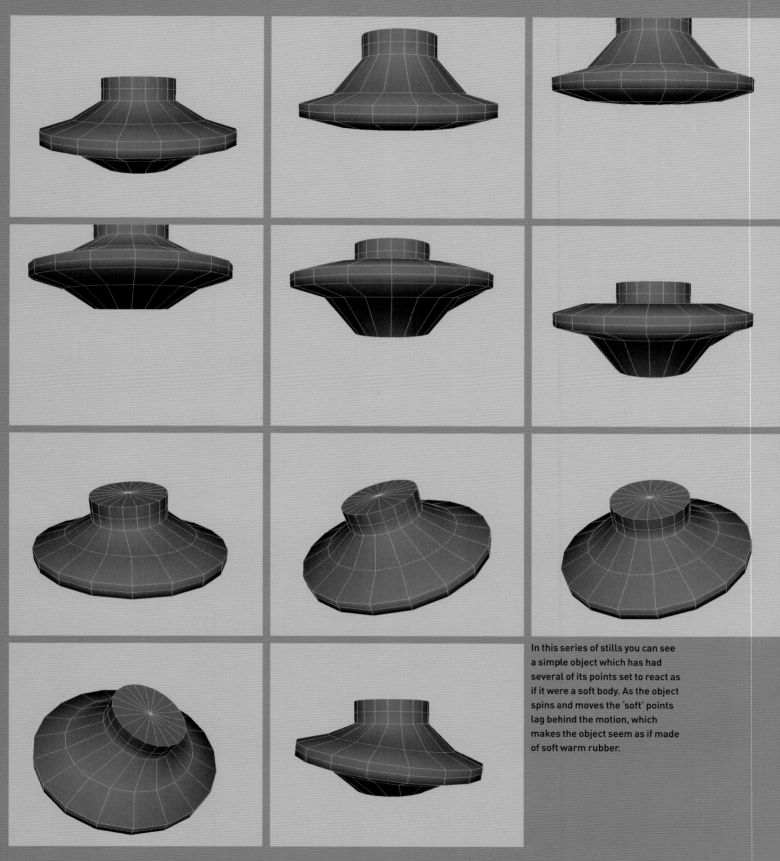

In this series of stills you can see a simple object which has had several of its points set to react as if it were a soft body. As the object spins and moves the 'soft' points lag behind the motion, which makes the object seem as if made of soft warm rubber.

BROADCAST GRAPHICS In the world of broadcast media, 3D has become essential for creating titles and graphics for programs and live events. It seems that no sports coverage is complete without some spinning, glittery, animated graphic or a flashy 3D scorecard.

3D now has a place in nearly every kind of program, from quick visualizations in sports programs to animated characters in children's shows. The downside of the popularity of 3D graphics and animation in broadcast media is that some visual styles quickly become hackneyed. Luckily, traditional flying logos and shiny spinning letters are slowly being replaced by a more subtle merging of 2D and motion graphics with 3D elements that doesn't scream CGI at you. It is a sure sign that audiences are becoming increasingly accustomed to the use of 3D and that their taste for it is becoming more sophisticated. The pressure is on for ever better graphics and animations.

Left: Traditional flying logos can be easily created in any 3D program. For broadcasting they need to be rendered at the native resolution and frame rate of the broadcast medium. In the US the NTSC format has a resolution of 704 x 480 pixels and runs at 30 frames per second. The PAL format used in the UK and most of Europe has a slightly higher 720 x 576 pixel resolution, but runs at a slower 25 frames per second.

Left: 3D animations destined for the TV must also be rendered to take account of the fields of the broadcasting systems. Television systems don't display whole frames one after another; rather they display them using a process called interlacing. First the even rows of pixels are displayed, then the odd rows. Since each odd and even row is shown alternately at 50Hz (NTSC) you effectively double the frame rate, albeit at technically half the resolution. Because of the persistence of vision phenomenon and the speed of the scan rate, we don't register this flickering of the image between odd and even fields. A video still containing moving objects will show the fields clearly, however. When rendering in 3D you can usually save fields rather than whole frames.

part 02. 3D in the real world

Left: 3D characters can be found hosting TV programmes, in commercials and channel identifiers and often in children's television programmes. Simple 3D characters are ideal for children's TV, continuing the trend set by traditional cel-animation.

Left: Graphs and charts are a typical subject for 3D news graphics. With bold colours, clean lines and animation, statistical information can be given an interesting visual makeover.

3D DIGITAL VIDEO EFFECTS DVEs (Digital Video Effects) give motion graphics artists and video editors a huge range of creative possibilities when it comes to designing broadcasting visuals. Most motion-graphics and video-editing programs come with a 3D plug-in of some description, which lets you wrap video images around 3D surfaces, perform sophisticated 3D transformations and layer video clips in new and imaginative ways.

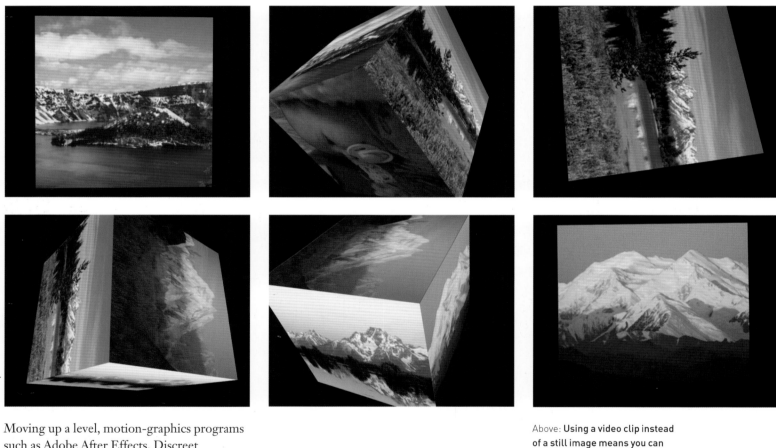

Moving up a level, motion-graphics programs such as Adobe After Effects, Discreet Combustion and Apple Shake now integrate near-full 3D environments in what is still technically a 2D domain. These programs offer varying degrees of 3D freedom – some even have lights and cameras like a 3D program. These are usually more difficult to work with in 3D however, which is why 3D programs make ideal complementary tools for DVE work.

Above: **Using a video clip instead of a still image means you can perform sophisticated DVEs in a 3D program. A classic example is the video cube. Each face of this cube has a different video clip assigned to it. During the animation the cube spins, playing the video clips as it does so.**

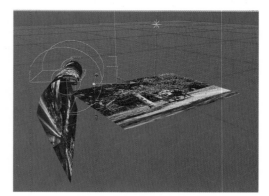

Above left to right: **Another classic DVE is the page curl. Although it has been overused (to say the least) it's a good effect to demonstrate how DVEs are done in a 3D package. In this example a page curl is used to make the transition between one clip and another. Two planes are positioned one on top of the other, and an ambient light is added to the scene and set to 100 per cent so that the video planes display without any shading.**

A bend deformer is applied to the topmost plane, which is heavily subdivided, with a bend angle of 270°. As the bend deformer is moved across the scene, it curls up the plane revealing the one below.

The reason the bend is 270° is so that the bent plane does not become visible when it curls over. If a 180° or 360° bend is used then the plane will become visible again as the bend passes though it. With a 270° bend the excess part of the plane travels vertically downwards through the plane at the bottom.

Above: **By rendering from a non-perspective top view, the effect appears seamless. You could animate the bend at any speed, or change its angle and direction to create variations of the same effect. This is just the tip of the iceberg, of course – the sky is the limit with 3D DVEs.**

WEB 3D It's usually only 3D artists and gamers who get to experience interactive 3D graphics. Displaying rich 3D content on a computer can be demanding on system hardware, which is one reason why 3D graphics on the Web have taken a while to become established. Another is that, generally speaking, the data required to render a moderate 3D scene is quite large. However, this is changing. The proliferation of broadband Internet access means that rich Web content, including large graphics, animation and 3D on the Web is a reality for many users.

There are many different Web technologies and standards in use on the Web, with numerous companies supplying their own brand of 3D content deployment, compression and display software. There are a few different schemes involved but the one that is emerging as favourite is where a Web browser plug-in renders and displays the raw 3D data that is downloaded. This allows maximum compression of the data while in transit, and most of the hard work of creating the 3D scene is handled on the fly at the receiver's computer.

However, Web 3D graphics still seem to be limited to certain markets and genres, and typical Web users may have never even come across a site containing interactive 3D. If they do, they will most likely have to download a plug-in of viewer, just as if they wanted to view a site enabled with Shockwave or Flash. Thankfully many of these viewers have reduced in size from one or two megabytes to a few hundred kilobytes, making installation a pretty painless process, even through a dial-up connection.

Two popular Web 3D technologies include Viewpoint VET and Shockwave 3D. In order to create Shockwave or Viewpoint 3D content you need to install an export plug-in for your particular 3D application. Most of the big 3D apps are supported, so it's relatively simple to create scenes and deploy them on your site.

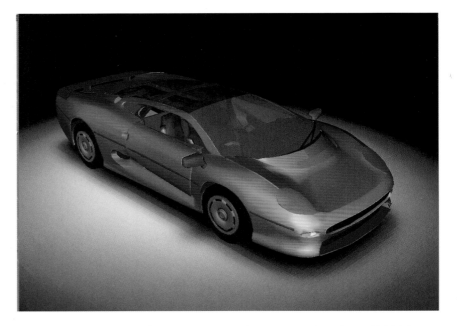

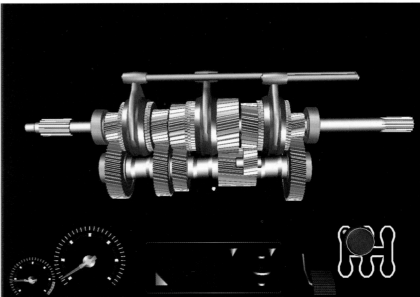

Above right: **Cortona is a VRML-based Web 3D system by Parallel Graphics.** Users can download the viewer for free to view 3D-enabled websites. There are many different developers and technologies for using 3D on the Web, so if you come across a site using a different system you may need to download a specific 3D viewer.

Right: **When viewing Web 3D content, you generally have a screen in a Webpage, which you can manipulate by dragging.** The controls offered differ depending on what has been implemented for that scene and what is supported by the 3D system itself. You will usually be able to rotate, pan, and zoom the view as a minimum.

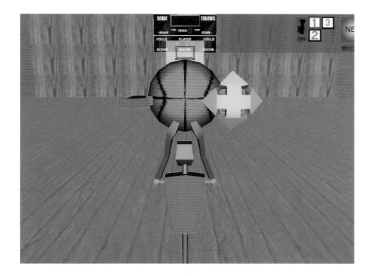

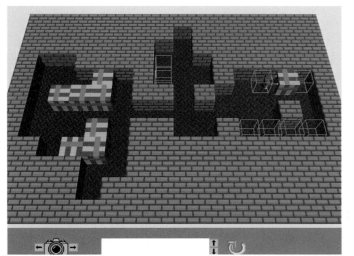

Left: **Using the same technology for viewing objects interactively, Web designers can add interactivity to create simple 3D games. Two games are shown here, Basketball (41KB) and Socoban (10KB). The graphics are very simple so the download size is tiny.**

Right: **By taking photographs of real locations and using them as texture maps on simple geometry, you can create virtual environments based on real locations. This, for example, is Montmartre in Paris.**

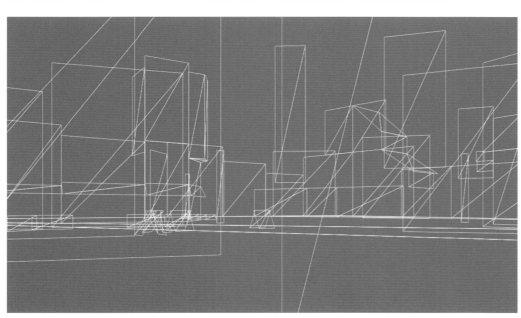

Left: **The geometry of this scene is extremely simple, and at only 4.2KB it represents a near instant download. It's the textures that take longer, but with careful preparation even these can be reduced to a mere 600KB or so.**

2D TO 3D

03

2D CANVAS AND 3D SPACE

Getting to grips with working in 3D can be difficult, especially if you are used to the 2D canvas offered in traditional painting and drawing applications. With 2D art, what you see is what you get: you are directly creating the final image as you work in Adobe Photoshop, Illustrator or whatever program takes your fancy. In 3D the workflow is quite different. You begin by building the elements that make up the final artwork (or animation) but the actual image itself doesn't come together until quite late in the process. Therefore, working on a 3D scene takes a certain degree of planning and forethought: otherwise you can waste a lot of time working on parts that ultimately contribute little to the final image.

The other big difference between 2D and 3D workflows is that the tools are more abstract in 3D than in a 2D program. In Photoshop, say, you have tools that correspond directly to the finished artwork – a brush, a pen, a clone tool, etc. They are all used to work

on the final image itself so there is a logical relationship and directness between the tools and the artwork. In 3D the tools can seem bizarre, awkward or nonsensical and they don't always relate to the finished image in any way. It is this very sense of being at one remove from the artwork that many 2D artists struggle with when they first migrate to 3D.

However, it's something that you do get used to, like moving a pointer with a mouse while you're looking at a computer screen. 3D artists are always thinking ahead – imagining how what they are currently working on will work in the finished scene – and this is a skill that can be learnt with practice.

The other problem 2D artists face is how to transfer from a flat world of two dimensions to the infinite void of three. Thankfully most 3D work is done on flat planes, too, even when working in a full 3D environment.

Opposite: **Painting on a 2D canvas is simple because you are using a 2D input device (a mouse or pen) to control 2D tools. But when you watch a 3D artist working on a model in a 3D-perspective view, it can be difficult to grasp what's going on. While it may seem that work is being done in three dimensions, that's usually not the case.**

Right: **If a 3D artist decides to move a point on a 3D model, he first selects it. Handles are displayed that indicate the three axes of movement, X, Y and Z, and by dragging one handle at a time the movement of the point is constrained to that single direction.**

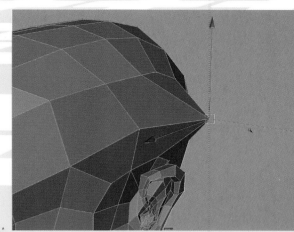

Left: **While an artist may be viewing or rotating a model in 3D, the actual work of modeling is often done in one or two dimensions at a time. This is because it is impossible to use a 2D input device such as a mouse or graphics tablet to input 3D data accurately. By using a set of axes to control the movement of points, polygons or objects, the 3D artists can limit the movement either to a plane or along a specific axis, despite viewing the scene in 3D. Models are usually built facing a particular axis so they are correctly aligned to begin with.**

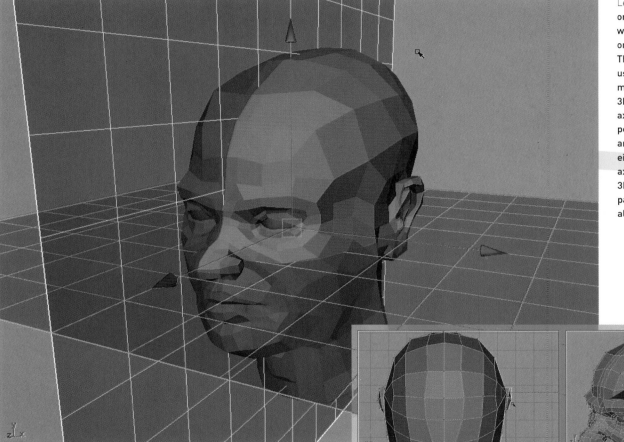

Right: **By rotating the view around after each edit, you can more easily tell where in 3D space the point is and adjust its position one axis at a time. Alternatively, viewing three orthogonal views at once shows you the position of the point along the three axes, which makes correct positioning very easy.**

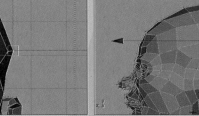

PERSPECTIVE Until about 1400 AD perspective was poorly understood. Prior to this, some attempts were made at recreating its effects but the rules governing it proved hard to grasp. The earliest perspective paintings had lines converging at different points in the distance, causing objects to look distorted. They still worked as artistic images, but technically speaking they were incorrect.

A 3D program can generate accurate perspective automatically without your having to work it out, but it still helps to understand the principle of perspective and how it can be created in 2D. Thinking about every aspect of a design including those that the computer calculates for you, can be beneficial in terms of the clarity of your design.

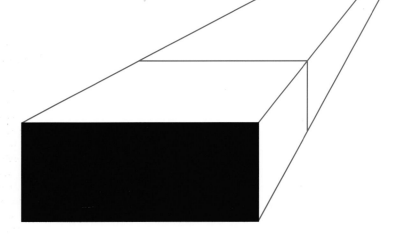

Above: **Simple perspective can be calculated by defining a vanishing point and extending all straight lines to this one point. The vanishing point is the point on the horizon where it appears that parallel lines converge. Of course they don't really converge – it's just the effect of objects shrinking in size as they get farther from us. You can draw straight-sided objects using this method, but it's not totally accurate as only one set of parallel edges of a cube is used to generate the perspective; the other lines remain parallel in the drawing. One-point perspective generates objects that have one side facing directly towards us.**

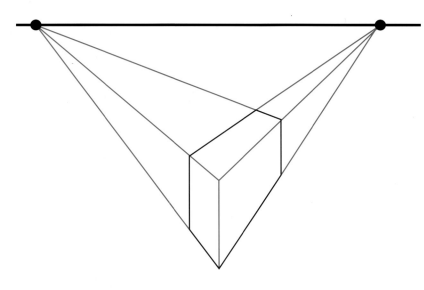

Left: Two-point perspective is created by using two sets of parallel lines on a cube or block. It can be used to create objects that are not directly facing the viewer. Instead of a single vanishing point, two are chosen, and corresponding edges are extended to these points of reference. The closer together these points, the more dramatic the perspective.

Left: The most complicated to draw, three-point perspective utilizes all three sets of parallel edges of a cube and three vanishing points, and it requires at least one of these not to lie on the horizon. Constructing a cube involves drawing the six sets of lines connecting the cube's edges to the vanishing points. The resulting object is seen rotated at 45° and from above by about 35°. It's also possible to generate four- and five-point perspective. These result in curved lines and can be used to simulate very wide-angle views of up to 180°.

SIMULATING 3D IN 2D Despite the power, flexibility and complexity of 3D programs, it's still possible to do great 3D work in a 2D program. After all, painters have been creating realistic pseudo-3D images for centuries using tools far less sophisticated than the average 2D image-editor. By taking the behaviour of light, materials, surfaces and perspective into account, you can easily create near-photoreal results in Adobe Photoshop alone.

This example is a humorous image created entirely in Photoshop. It makes use of techniques and analysis that would also be done in a 3D program to achieve realism, but it maintains a 2D style all of its own.

Below: Then the fish scale textures are overlaid on top...

Bottom: Finally shading is applied, taking into account that a fish is partially translucent. Note that you get the impression of a backbone through the skin, and that the body, which is less obscured by bones, is bright orange because more light can pass. The head which has thicker bone, is a red-orange colour. Interestingly, these are the same things you would bear in mind if you tried to create the same image in a 3D program.

Above: You don't need a raytracer to create glass reflections. The glass bowl sports two large window reflections that are simple 2D shapes overlaid on the image. Subtle use of masking provides Fresnel fall-off for the reflected shapes just as it would in a 3D render. Remove the reflections, and the glass bowl instantly looks fake.

Above right: The effects of light play a big part in determining the look of an object's surface. Translucency is the key to getting the fish to look right, and all it needs is some time with a digital paintbrush. The fish begins its life as a flat shape.

Below right: Then some colour is added...

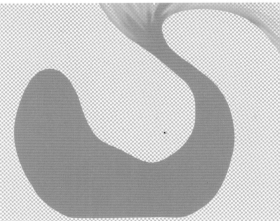

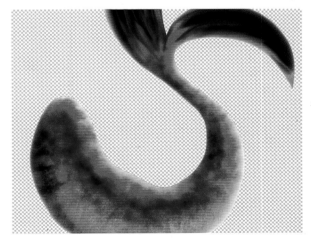

SPATIAL AWARENESS AND DESIGNING IN 3D Spatial awareness is important for the creation of realistic 3D images. Being able to rotate, transform and dissect forms in your imagination is essential for drawing figures and objects correctly, no matter what environment they are created in. In some ways this ability is more important for 2D artists than 3D artists, because as long as you are methodical, the computer will always maintain the spatial relationships of objects when working in a 3D program.

Drawing on a 2D canvas can be more demanding because you have to build spatial information into your image by hand, often working out complex perspective solutions as you go. Some artists just have a feel for it, and whether in 2D or 3D their work always looks good.

Above right: **Spatial awareness is also crucial when designing a 3D object. The idea may start in your head but it'll often still require some sketching before the proportions and the relationships between parts of the model look good. Here's a sketch of a plasma-cannon design created by Brian Pace.**

Right: **Once the design is sketched a model can begin to be built in 3D. It doesn't always have to be done like this, since some 3D artists can sketch directly in 3D, but a pen and paper is usually quicker for trying design ideas out. Next is an image of a simplified version of the model in 3D. The key design elements are in place and the overall form and proportion looks good. Unlike a 2D sketch the 3D design can be rotated and viewed from all angles – this will help to show up any weak areas of the model.**

Opposite top: **Once the design is settled, the 3D artist can work on the model until the desired level of detail is achieved, adding textures and lighting for a final render.**

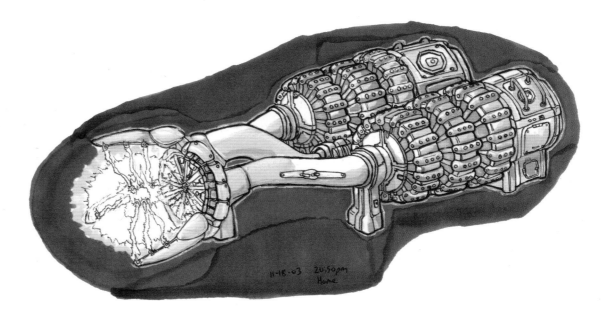

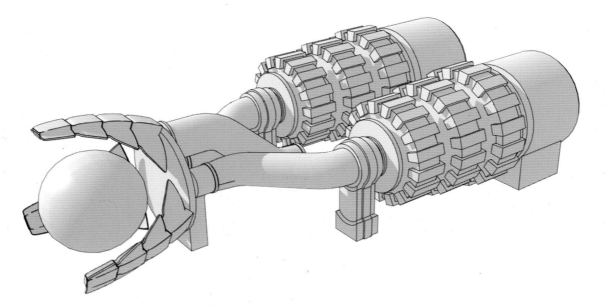

part 03. 2D to 3D

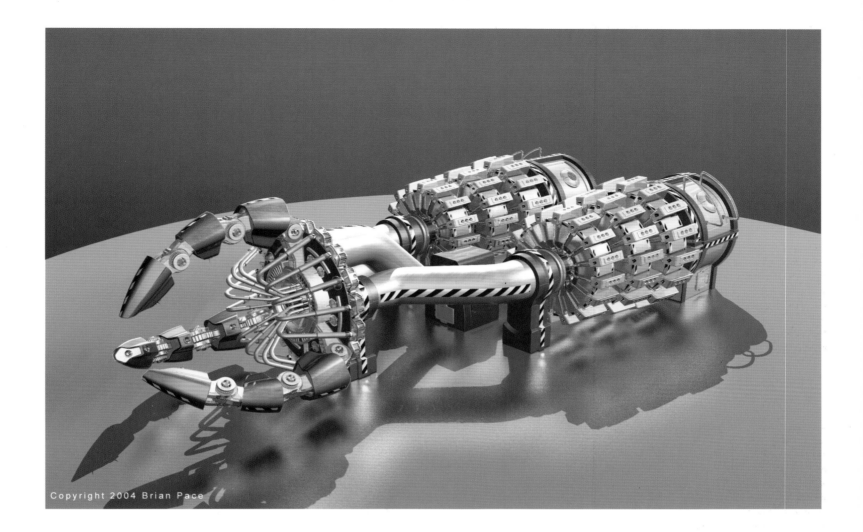

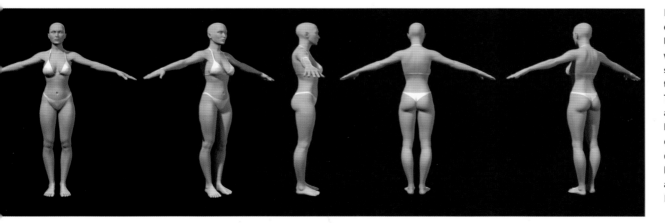

Left: When building 3D models, especially very complicated ones like human characters, 3D artists will rotate the object using a shaded view so that they can grasp the form of the object in their mind. The computer monitor only displays a 2D image so this constant rotation back and forth helps to make the object a little more three-dimensional. It's as if the artist is holding the object and turning it around to look at it from all sides.

Dan Phillips, http://dcp.lihp.com

RECREATING PHOTOREALITY A lot of 3D work involves realism. The term you'll often hear used is 'photorealistic' when discussing such work. There's a difference between photorealism and plain old realism, and that has a lot to do both with the way 3D programs are designed and the ultimate use of the 3D images.

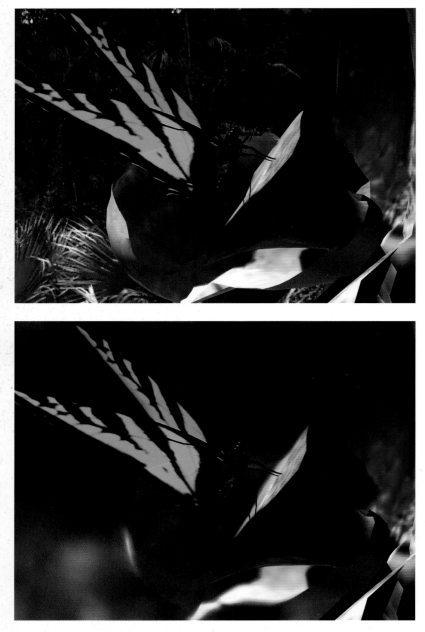

3D programs are designed around the concept of the camera. Because much 3D work is intended either to match images already photographed or replace them (such as in visual effects or visualization) the photo aspect of photorealism is key to achieving seamless and believable results.

When a camera takes an image, it captures light by focusing it onto a photographic film or light-sensitive CCD chip. It's a similar system to our eyesight, but one that's not quite as well designed or sophisticated. As a result the camera/lens system is prone to many kinds of visual quirks and artefacts, and simulating these is often key to achieving photorealistic results in 3D. However, it can require lots of effort to get these artefacts to work convincingly in a scene.

One quirk is to do with the way that the lens of a camera focuses – a quality known as depth of field. When the lens aperture is opened up wide (particularly in low-light situations), the focal distance is reduced. Objects closer to and farther from the point of sharp focus appear blurred. When focusing on a subject very close to the camera, this depth-of-field blurring can be very pronounced. In fact, some modern photographic techniques involve tilting the film plane relative to the lens to achieve an even more pronounced, artificial depth blurring.

Left above: **Depth-of-field blurring is an artistic device that you can make use of in 3D work. If you want to emulate close-up macro photography, making use of the depth-of-field feature in most 3D programs can give your renders that photoreal quality. Without DOF rendering this image is fine, but it lacks realism. The fact that everything is in sharp focus actually makes it oddly confusing.**

Left: **By enabling DOF rendering and setting up the camera so that the butterfly is at the point of perfect focus, the render is much more realistic. It's also a more pleasing composition, because the busy background has been blurred.**

Above: Another artefact is lens flare. This occurs when bright light enters the lens at a shallow angle and causes obscuring reflections within the lens system. Photographers try to avoid this by using lens hoods to prevent stray light entering the lens, but it can also be used creatively.

Left: In 3D, lens flare can be simulated. It is usually defined per light as opposed to per camera. This allows you to control exactly which light is to produce a flare. A great effect is produced when an object passes in front of a light that has a flare, causing the flare to cut in and out. This adds a tremendous amount to certain 3D animations – if used sparingly.

SHADOWS AND LIGHT Light and shadow play an important role in any image, whether generated in a computer, created by hand or photographed. Because you have to position and set up lights as if they were real objects when creating a 3D image, it is important to understand the roles that light and shade play in an image, or you risk getting carried away by the technicalities of the lighting rig itself.

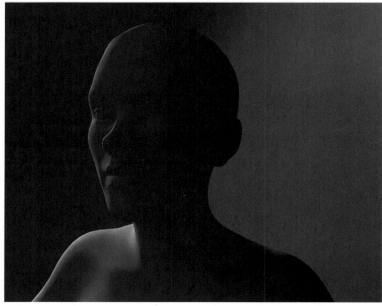

It's very easy to get 3D lighting wrong. It can take a lot of trial and error to get to grips with designing a 3D lighting rig, making it easy to overlook the artistic impact light can have. It's interesting to note that, by and large, 2D artists begin with a white canvas and add shading to it to create objects and images. A 3D environment is totally black to begin with and the process is reversed – in a sense you are adding darkness to the image. As you add lights, you define areas of illumination as opposed to areas of shadow. This is where many novices make their mistake – it's all too easy to over-illuminate.

It's not necessary to illuminate the whole surface of an object; this is especially true for animations. The object has to be readable, and for that, well-defined edges are essential. When you sketch with a pencil and paper, you generally start with edges and add the shading. Even a rough sketch can read very well with well-chosen lines and shading. The same approach can be taken with 3D.

Opposite, top left: **This image has too much illumination.** There are only two lights used but they have washed out the image, resulting in very little shading and a lack of tonal balance in the image. The shadows are not well placed either. There's very little interest in the image because the lighting gives everything away and does not show the object off well.

Opposite, top right: **This image is more interesting.** The lighting is almost nonexistent, with two lights as before, but this time one is a very low-value fill, the other a bright light positioned behind and to the side so that only a sliver of light catches her face. The artist is not attempting to illuminate the surface of the model at all, but trying to show the edges. However, only one side of the model is delineated. How can we do the same to the other side without making her brighter?

Opposite, bottom: **Simple. Add** another light but shine it on the background only. Now the side of the model not illuminated has been delineated as a silhouette against the brighter background. Using a spotlight, it is relatively easy to aim the illumination so that none is cast behind the bright side of her head. One side is black against white, the other white against black.

Below: **The same technique can** work well for multiple subjects. In this example, one character is lit brightly against a black background while the other is in shadow against a light background. The lighting can be reversed to suggest a different mood or change the emphasis between the subjects.

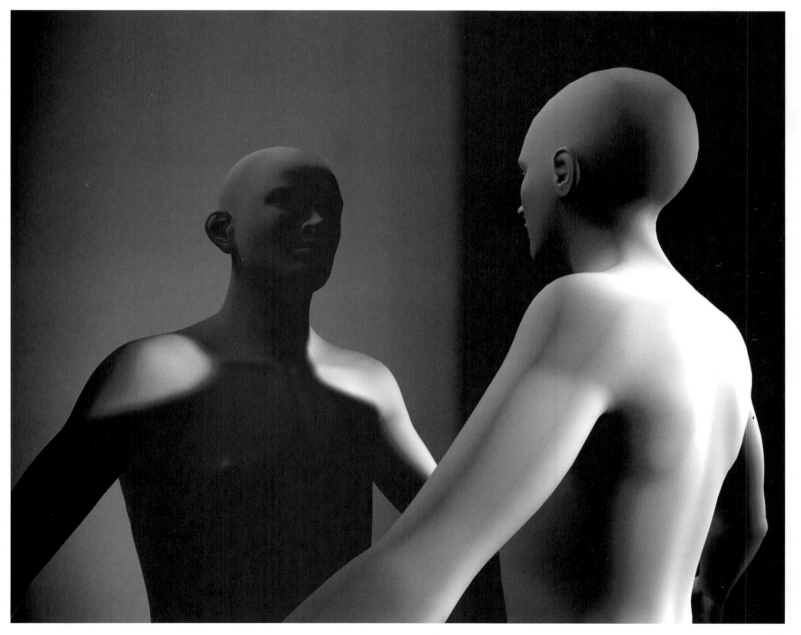

3D CORE CONCEPTS

04

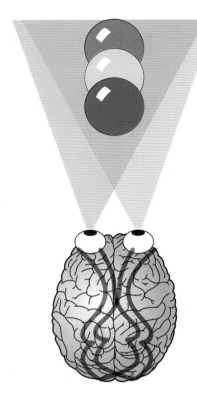

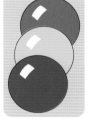

THE NATURE OF 3D

At the most fundamental level, digital 3D graphics offer a visual simulation of the physical world in which we live. Although they are sometimes confused with the term 'virtual reality', they are not the same thing. However, this link with reality is important. Once you break down the core of what makes 3D graphics tick, you come to understand the ways in which 3D graphics relate to reality.

Currently digital 3D graphics are used intensively in a limited number of fields, including the entertainment industry, engineering and design, architecture and even the world of fine art. Their use in virtual reality systems has so far been limited, simply because it's still not possible to create truly believable, fully immersive graphics at the display rate required – in real time. Affordable computers aren't powerful enough yet. However 3D technology and computing power are slowly eroding this barrier, and it is conceivable that in the future 3D graphics will play a greater role in our lives.

This may actually have important moral and philosophical implications in the future, as digital 3D becomes ever more proficient at simulating reality. We are already at the stage when 3D artists can create still images that are indistinguishable from photographs, and these artists can do so in very little time. Of course, the image created by 3D software is a 2D image, but the same goes for the image formed on our retina by the lens of our eye. It's only our stereoscopic vision that adds the sense of depth. Perhaps technology in the future will let us feed digital 2D digital images directly into our brain, or scan them directly onto our corneas. How easy will it be for us to tell if what we are looking at is real or generated?

Above: **We see because light is focused by our corneas, at the front of the eyes, onto the back to form a 2D image. We see in 3D because our eyes take in the scene from slightly different viewpoints. Our brain reconciles the two eye images in a single 3D image.**

Left: As digital 3D increases in its ability to capture the subtle nuances of reality, it's getting harder and harder to tell the difference between what's real and what is computer generated, as this image shows. There's no evidence to suggest this trend will cease, and in the future it may be impossible to tell what is real and what isn't.

Above: *Mousetrapped* by Studio 3D. (www.studio3D.com). By rendering the same scene from slightly different positions, it's possible to create left- and right-eye image pairs digitally. The tricky part is feeding one image to one eye only, and the other image to the other eye only. Research is taking place into creating true stereoscopic 3D displays without the need for 3D glasses, but it's still a long way from becoming a practical reality. Instead, we use glasses to filter the image. One method uses glasses with polarizing lenses, which alternately become opaque then transparent, connected to a display that alternates between the right and left image in time with the glasses. Do this quickly enough and the result is a 3D image.

Below: This is the same scene, but this time there are no lights as such. The illumination is created using a large self-luminous plane object. When rendered using radiosity, the bright surface of the plane acts as a light source illuminating the scene. This technique requires high quality radiosity settings to achieve the same results as normal 3D lights together with radiosity.

Below: The same technique can be used for exterior scenes. Using a large luminous 'skydome' encompassing the scene you can create realistic ambient exterior illumination. Combine this with a normal distant light to simulate the sun, and you can create a good approximation of real-world outside lighting. In this example a blue material on the skydome simulates the diffuse blue light from the Earth's atmosphere, while the distant light provides direct illumination – here it's orange, to simulate a rising sun.

Currently many modern 3D programs offer adaptive radiosity technology that, like adaptive raytracing, reduces the rendering time by varying the quality of the radiosity algorithm over the image.

Because radiosity takes the brightness of surfaces into account when calculating scene illumination, it's possible to eliminate lights entirely. By making an object self-luminous, giving it a material with the Luminosity/Ambient channel set to full brightness, objects in the scene can act as light sources.

SUBSURFACE SCATTERING Radiosity isn't the only advancement in rendering. While radiosity takes into account the light bounced between objects in a scene, subsurface scattering (SSS for short) deals with light that bounces around below an object's surface.

Many objects that seem opaque actually have a degree of translucency. Light can pass a few millimetres into the top layers of many materials and is scattered by the substance the object is made of, creating a degree of diffuse illumination below the surface of the object. Skin is a good example and one we are all familiar with. Hold a strong torch behind your fingers and you'll see a red glow, which gets brighter at the edges of your fingers. This is the effect that SSS replicates.

Even in normal lighting situations this scattered light beneath the surface affects the appearance of objects, and we can detect it. You only need to see a render from a 3D program that doesn't have SSS rendering features to see how true this is. When you want to create objects made from plastics, wax, quartz and other diaphanous materials, subsurface scattering is absolutely essential. Even materials such as marble and other stones benefit from this effect. Trying to recreate even a simple glass of milk in 3D can prove fruitless without SSS rendering. However, like raytracing and radiosity, the intense calculations involved in subsurface scattering take time.

Below left: A render of an object without subsurface scattering and with just two light sources, above and to the left of the object.

Below right: When *Subsurface Scattering* is turned on in the object's *Material*, a startling transformation occurs. The light permeates the volume of the object, giving it a semi-translucent appearance. This is an extreme example; SSS is just as effective when used subtly.

Left: Candle wax is a good example of a substance that scatters light and is translucent. With SSS enabled for the wax materials, the candle becomes more believable. Notice that a lot of the colour of the wax comes through absorption of certain wavelengths of light; the colour gets deeper, the farther in the light travels.

Below: Without SSS enabled, as in this image, the candle looks OK but the effect is not so realistic. The light and the surface don't react as we expect them to.

ARTIST'S TOOLKIT

05

PART 05. ARTIST'S TOOLKIT

CHAPTER ONE

ESSENTIAL TOOLS

To work in 3D, you need to have hardware that is up to the job. Luckily, that is no longer such a tall order. In the early days you would have spent thousands of pounds on Unix workstations and high-end software to equip yourself with a powerful 3D system. Now your average Mac or PC is more than up to the job.

Traditionally, the Apple Macintosh was not held in high regard in 3D circles. In part this was due to a lack of interest in the 3D market by Apple at the time, and because the Mac's operating system (the core software that controls the computer) was not modern enough for professional 3D work. As a result, few 3D programs were developed for the Mac. Although the Mac's enduring appeal for digital artists kept a small stock of exceptional 3D programs alive and kicking, Windows PCs took the lion's share of the 3D market. If you were serious about 3D, you bought a PC.

Things changed dramatically when Apple introduced its next-generation operating system, OS X. OS X was based on industry-standard Unix – the high-end 3D market's OS of choice – and this generated a huge revival in the Mac as a valid 3D platform. Now most of the high-end 3D programs have been ported to OS X, including the Maya, the industry leader. Combined with Apple's latest G5-processor Power Macs, the Mac has everything going for it for 3D.

Windows PCs remain the bedrock of high-end 3D design, and on the whole are slightly cheaper. The bottom line for many artists, however, is that Microsoft's Windows XP operating system lags behind Apple's OS X in terms of ease of use and interface design. In these terms, the Mac wins hands down every time.

The other crucial thing for 3D work – or indeed any kind of graphics work – is the robustness of the OS. After years of producing one version of Windows for home users – Windows 95, 98 or ME – and one for professionals – Windows NT or 2000 – Microsoft now has just one basic core, based on professional 32-bit NT kernel. As a result, both the Home and Professional versions of Windows XP have a solid foundation, and if you're not running either Windows 2000 or XP, you really should upgrade.

Similarly Apple's OS 9 will soon cease to be supported on new Macs, and it's not really suitable for 3D work anyway. Or rather, OS X is so much more advanced that it would be folly for your Mac not to run it. Any of the latest Macs, including the iMac G4, Powerbook G4 and Power Mac G5s, come with OS X already installed. Many older G3s can also run OS X, so it's worth upgrading these, too.

With XP and OS X you have protected memory, multi-processor support and pre-emptive multi-tasking. Although that sounds like technojargon, these are essential ingredients for a modern OS. With protected memory, for example, if one program crashes the system, all other programs will keep running. It's a fact of life that computer programs crash, so an OS that can protect your

hard work from a system-wide lock is essential. Multi-processing is also very useful because many computers, including some Apple Power Macs, feature multiple CPUs for faster performance.

In the end, however, the choice of Mac, PC or Unix platforms is not purely determined by how powerful or affordable the computer is, or how good the OS is. If you're serious about 3D design, your choice of 3D program should be the first determiner, since not all 3D programs run on all operating systems. 3ds max, for example, is Windows only and Houdini is available only for Unix and Windows. Maya Unlimited is also not available for OS X, though Maya Complete (missing a few of the high-end features like cloth and fur) does run on the Mac platform.

Left: **Apple's OS X is based on industrial-strength Unix, yet is easy to use, fast, powerful, very robust, and gaining a lot of ground in the 3D industry. The perfect OS for 3D artists? Probably.**

Right: **If you want to take advantage of relatively cheap PC hardware and can live without the cool design of OS X, then Windows is the way to go.**

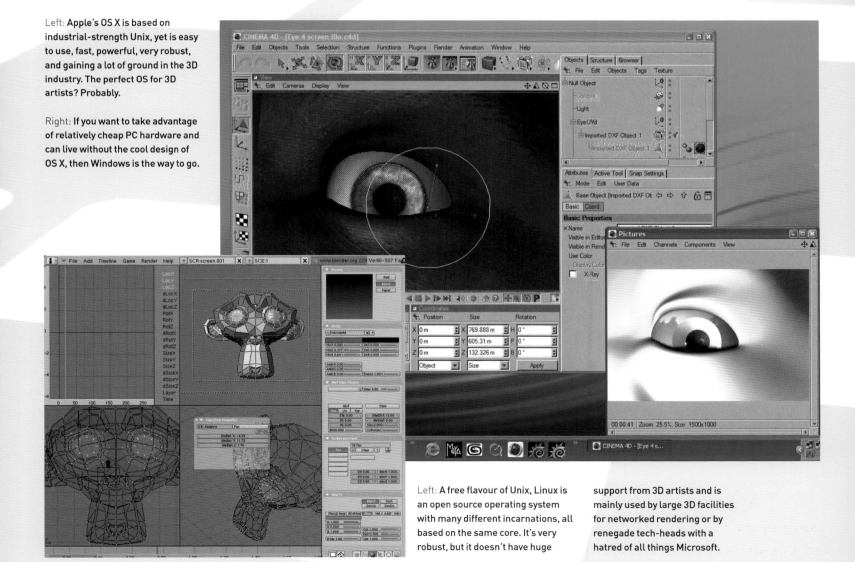

Left: **A free flavour of Unix, Linux is an open source operating system with many different incarnations, all based on the same core. It's very robust, but it doesn't have huge** support from 3D artists and is mainly used by large 3D facilities for networked rendering or by renegade tech-heads with a hatred of all things Microsoft.

WHAT YOU NEED TO DO 3D Once you've got past the basic question of OS, it's time to put a system together. 3D graphics is very CPU intensive, so it makes sense to get the fastest computer you can lay your hands on. If you are buying a machine specifically for 3D, you have the opportunity to create a system optimized for this demanding discipline, but most off-the-shelf PCs and Macs are perfectly suited to 3D work. These days, even some laptops can handle the workload.

Right: **Widescreen aspect ratio LCDs, such as the Apple Cinema Display, can support huge resolutions up to 1,680 x 1,050, giving you lots of space at the edge of the screen for command palettes and toolbars.**

Below: **CRT monitors are gradually being superseded by flat LCD screens. They are still widely used and a decent 19-inch CRT monitor can be purchased quite cheaply these days.**

Just make sure that you have enough RAM. For 3D work, 256Mb should be considered a minimum, 512Mb is highly recommended and 1Gb of RAM isn't excessive.

Obviously, processor speed is important. If you're taking the Mac route, aim for a G5 processor if you can afford it, or as fast a G4 processor as you can manage if you can't. The graphics and memory subsystems are faster on the Power Mac systems than on their eMac or iMac equivalents, but the latter are still fast enough to work in 3D.

Finally, you're going to need a lot of storage space. In terms of hard-disk space, consider 40Gb the minimum for notebooks and 80Gb the minimum for desktop systems. 120Gb or above would be a sensible choice. Likewise, some sort of backup is a must. Some people prefer an external hard drive, others prefer to burn work to CD using a built-in CD-RW drive, and as files get bigger a recordable/rewritable DVD drive looks more and more useful. In any case, it's a good idea to have something: there's nothing worse than losing all the data for a major project just before it's due for submission.

For a PC, aim for a Pentium 4 running at a minimum of 2.6GHz with Intel's speedy HyperThreading technology, or an AMD Athlon XP or Athlon 64 processor rated at 2.6GHz or above. Like the G5, the Athlon 64 is a 64-bit processor, which means it's ready for Microsoft's 64-bit desktop version of Windows XP, when it arrives.

We'll go into graphics cards on the next page, but one with 64Mb of texture RAM will work well. Look for 128Mb or more if you need to display a lot of textures in OpenGL at once.

Computer monitors are the next big concern, but don't necessarily think you need the biggest screen available to work efficiently in 3D. In professional desktop publishing (DTP) or graphics, where a monitor needs to be able to display entire double page spreads, 21-inch or 22-inch CRTs (Cathode Ray Tube screens) are commonplace. However, 3D work can be done on a much smaller screen space, and – believe it or not – the most popular choice for 3D artists is a 19-inch screen, closely followed by a 17-inch monitor. The benefit a small screen offers is a smaller footprint and affordability. A minimum of 1,024 x 786 resolution gives enough screen space for most 3D programs, though a 17-inch screen can be coaxed into running at 1,152 x 864, and 1,280 x 1,024 happily fits on most 19-inch screens without inducing eye strain.

LCD screens are an alternative to big, bulky, flickery CRTs, but are usually more expensive. The cost is coming down, however, and an LCD screen is ideal for 3D work, because it's flicker-free and much, much crisper. This reduces eye strain and fatigue.

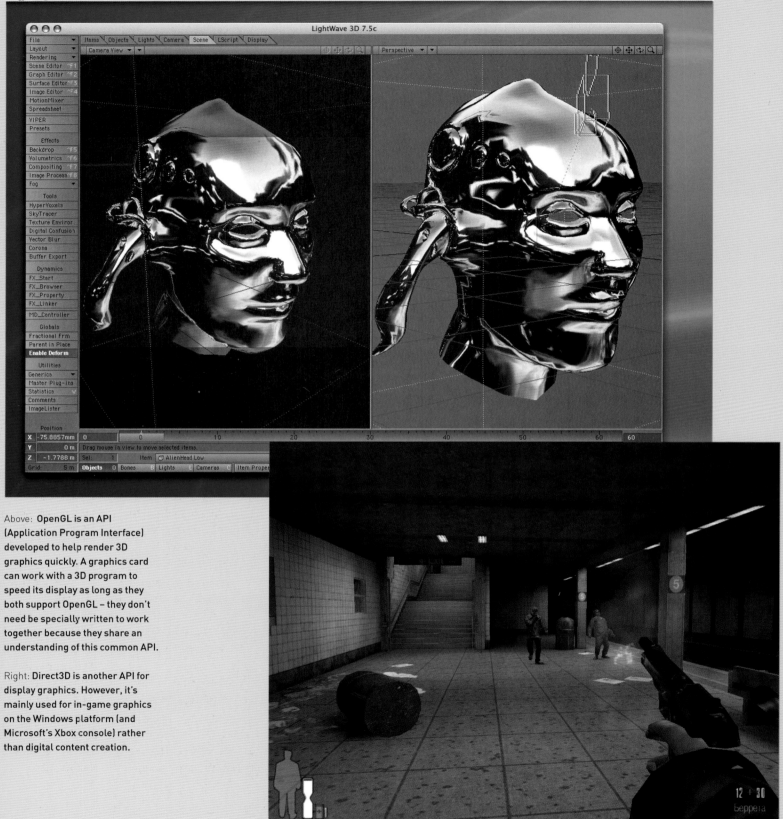

Above: **OpenGL is an API**
(Application Program Interface)
developed to help render 3D
graphics quickly. A graphics card
can work with a 3D program to
speed its display as long as they
both support OpenGL – they don't
need be specially written to work
together because they share an
understanding of this common API.

Right: **Direct3D is another API for**
display graphics. However, it's
mainly used for in-game graphics
on the Windows platform (and
Microsoft's Xbox console) rather
than digital content creation.

GRAPHICS CARDS AND APIS The graphics capabilities of a computer are an important consideration for 3D, as you might expect. There are two aspects to graphics hardware that can end up causing confusion, and a lot of this confusion is down to marketing.

Despite what manufacturers of 3D cards would have you believe, the speed of the computer's CPU and the amount of RAM installed are still the most important factors in serious 3D graphics, because these affect how fast the 3D program runs and how fast it renders. The graphics card, or the 3D-accelerator card, is still important – it's just that it's not as important unless you're playing games.

When you're working in 3D graphics, the graphics card powers the display graphics, not the final render, so any impact it has is restricted to the speed at which a 3D program displays the 3D scene as a work in progress. That's still significant: working on a 3D scene does require interactivity, so the faster the graphics card, the faster the display and the faster you can work. However, this is not a linear relationship, and there comes a point where the speed of the card will have minimal effect on the work you can do.

Cutting-edge 3D cards will fetch a high premium, too, so in the long term, the money may be better spent on CPU power. Mid-range 3D cards aimed at pro 3D users, such as those from nVIDIA or ATI, are a good choice, and you should also look at less expensive, game-oriented cards. These offer a

Above: **A graphics card accelerates the display of the 3D graphics on your computer. Games-oriented cards are good options if you are on a budget and will usually work well with most 3D programs. nVIDIA or ATI-based cards are the safest bet. Both companies have good relationships with the major software developers, and both have universal drivers, which can be downloaded from the appropriate website.**

good price/performance ratio, are supported by solid drivers and are usually based on the same fundamental technology.

Macs don't have the kind of support from third-party graphics card manufacturers that PCs do, but cards using nVIDIA and ATI chipsets are available and are suitable for all but the most demanding 3D scenes.

The important thing to remember is that a graphics card will not make renders go faster – they only improve the interactivity of the 3D display while you model and work with surfaces. There are two main technologies used to power display graphics: Direct3D (part of Microsoft's DirectX API) and SGI's OpenGL. Direct 3D is the choice for Windows-based gaming, but OpenGL is the de-facto standard in professional 3D graphics. Whatever card you choose, it should have full OpenGL support if you intend to work in 3D.

05.02

SOFTWARE

3D software tends to range in complexity and sophistication, although these days even the simplest 3D software is capable of impressive results. However, choosing the right 3D program is not a trivial matter, nor is it an easy one. There are many factors to take into account, and your choice will also depend on your intentions. Do you just want to dabble or include a little 3D rendering in your website? Perhaps you are a 2D designer and want to start incorporating 3D in your illustration work. Maybe you have learned about 3D using free software and intend pursuing 3D as a career. Over the next few pages we'll look at the options available in three general sectors of the market: basic, intermediate and advanced. Most 3D programs are available as demo versions, so you can try them out and get a feel of how they work before committing any cash.

SOFTWARE: BASIC

At the bottom end of the market there are plenty of low-cost, easy-to-use 3D programs. Because of the low cost and small market share, this is a volatile sector, with 3D apps popping into and out of existence like quantum foam. Some of these apps last a little longer than normal, while others vanish without trace, so don't be surprised if any mentioned here are no longer available by the time you read this. Whatever the name, they all tend to follow the same basic path – making 3D as easy as possible, but without the power and finesse of the more expensive packages.

Above: **If you want something for nothing, there are a few freeware versions of 3D packages available. 3D Canvas from amabilis.com is a cut-down version of the company's commercial 3D packages. It's a fully functional 3D app but is** **probably more suited to the intermediate 3D users or keen beginners. There is a lot of free Mac 3D software available, too, but these packages tend to be more intermediate or advanced in nature.**

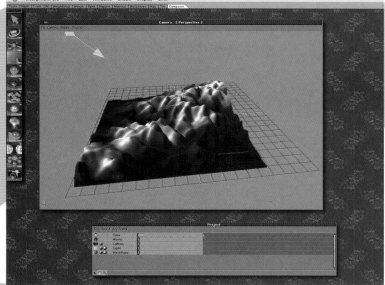

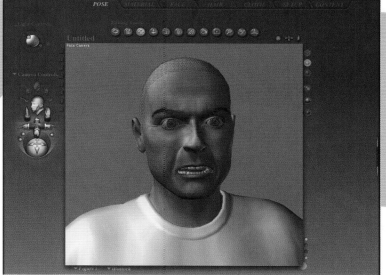

Top row, left to right: **Xara 3D** is a typical low-end 3D package, still going strong after multiple versions. Costing about £25, it's a PC-only 3D program that won't break the bank but is pretty limited as 3D programs go. Xara is great for quick logos and fun titles but that's really about it.

Adobe Dimensions is a plug-in for Illustrator (Mac or PC) that generates lit and rendered 3D objects from Illustrator curves and text. Again it's limited but very simple to use, and for some it's all that's needed.

Bottom row, left to right: Although more suited to intermediate users, **Amorphium** from ElectricImage Inc. is an easy-to-use 3D program designed to work in a very hands-on way. If you want to sculpt 3D objects as if they were lumps of clay then render them very simply, it is a good way to go.

Poser is included here because it is so easy to use, but in fact its usefulness extends right up to pro 3D work. It's a 3D character renderer and animator that lets you pose and animate ready-made, high-quality 3D figures. It's very powerful, but it's not an all-rounder: it does one thing only – but does it very well.

SOFTWARE: INTERMEDIATE Intermediate 3D software can be classed as packages that don't attempt to simplify 3D, but which let you access all aspects of a scene, from building models from scratch, to creating and modifying lights and textures, and rendering full resolution images or animations. There are lots of programs to choose from here, and nearly all of them are good. Some of the more notable offerings are listed here as an example of what to expect for your money. These programs have all been around for a few years in various incarnations and should continue to be so for the near future.

Right: This is the core application that forms the hub of Maxon's advanced 3D system. It can be bought on its own without the advanced plug-ins, and as such represents a fantastic bargain. It features a powerful modelling system, animation and fast rendering. It can be upgraded to the full advanced version simply by buying the plug-in modules.

www.maxon.net

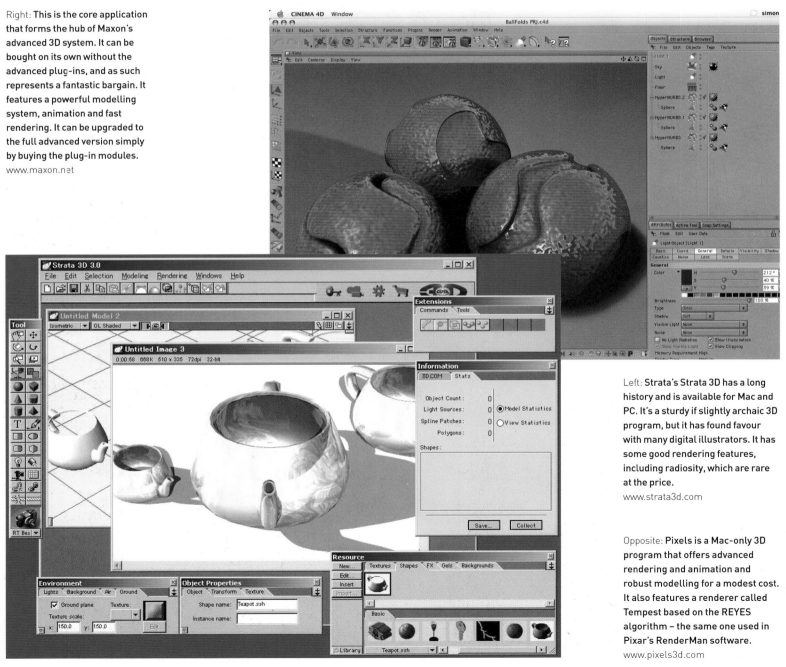

Left: Strata's Strata 3D has a long history and is available for Mac and PC. It's a sturdy if slightly archaic 3D program, but it has found favour with many digital illustrators. It has some good rendering features, including radiosity, which are rare at the price.

www.strata3d.com

Opposite: Pixels is a Mac-only 3D program that offers advanced rendering and animation and robust modelling for a modest cost. It also features a renderer called Tempest based on the REYES algorithm – the same one used in Pixar's RenderMan software.

www.pixels3d.com

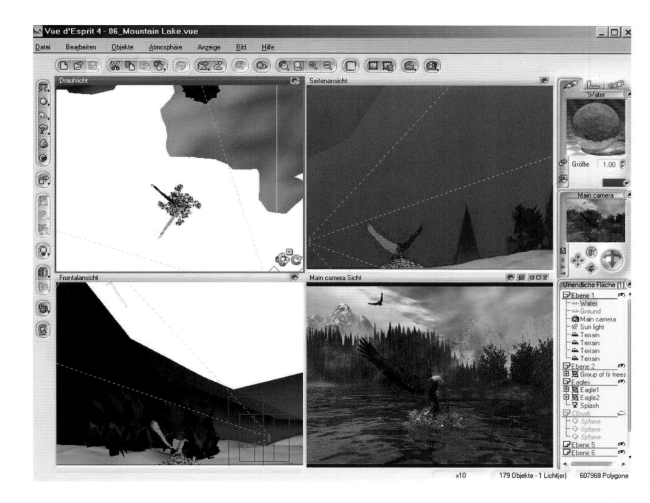

Left: Vue d'Esprit from E-on software is a landscape creation and rendering program along the same lines a Corel's Bryce 3D. It's a lot more powerful, however, and can generate impressive trees, shrubs and plants, too.
www.e-on.com

Below: Corel's Bryce 3D is an interesting 3D program. It's primarily a landscape-rendering application, designed to produce skys, seas and terrains in a very efficient way. It can be pressed into service as a more general-purpose 3D tool, too, but lacks any serious modelling tools.
www.corel.com

■ The quality of intermediate 3D software can vary, but there are a few things to bear in mind. Make sure the rendering is up to scratch, and examine on-line galleries of the software, which you can usually find on the developer's site. This will usually give you a good idea of the quality on offer. Most of the programs are available as demo versions so they can be downloaded for evaluation.

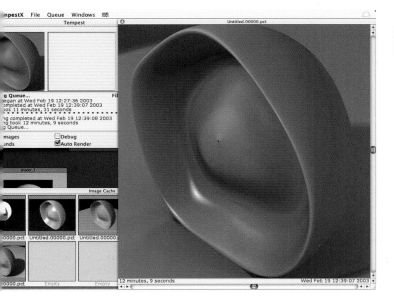

SOFTWARE: ADVANCED In the upper echelons of 3D graphics software, there is a group of five or six packages that define the state of the art of commercial 3D software. Most of these packages cost upwards of £1,000, and are full-featured 3D suites, capable of creating anything you can imagine. Actually that's the wrong way to put it. The high-end 3D programs are sophisticated tool sets that give 3D artists the freedom to create anything they can imagine and do so efficiently and to tight deadlines.

The key features of these apps is that elusive and hard-to-define quality, workflow. 3D is such a complex discipline that the methodology used throughout a 3D program, and its interface and design, have as much impact on the work as the technological features and tools themselves do. At the high-end it's not so much the tools as their implementation that makes the difference, and each 3D app has its own style of working.

These high-end 3D programs include Softimage | XSI, Discreet's 3ds max, Side Effects' Houdini, Newtek's Lightwave 3D, Alias' Maya and Maxon's Cinema 4D. There is another high-end package called PhotoRealistic RenderMan, which is a renderer, not a full software suite. However, RenderMan is arguably the most popular 3D renderer for high-end effects and is used together with the likes of Maya, XSI and Houdini in film and broadcast work. It's costly, seriously powerful and runs on IRIX, Linux and Windows operating systems, and has been announced for OS X as well.

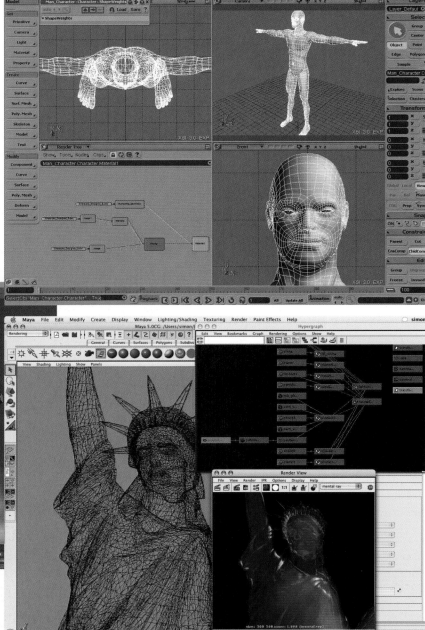

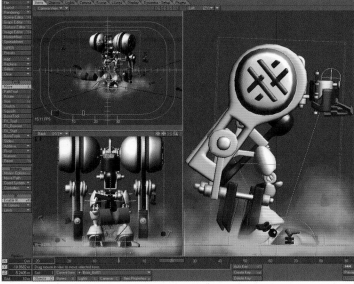

Above: **Newtek's Lightwave 3D is a dual application featuring separate modeller/texturing and animation/ lighting/rendering apps. Its quirky** interface is deceptively powerful, and it offers one of the best quality renderers you could hope for.
www.newtek.com

Below: **Discreet's 3ds max** has always been a popular choice. Its design is not as modern as Maya or Softimage | XSI but it holds its own, especially in the games production market, and comes with Mental Ray rendering as standard.

Right: **Houdini** is a fully procedural animation system that takes the node-based architecture to the nth degree. Sublimely powerful, it's not for the faint-hearted, but offers the kind of flexibility other apps only hint at.

Below: **The full suite of plug-ins for Cinema 4D** takes it into the high end. With advanced radiosity rendering, sophisticated character tools and a GUI-based expression system, it's also one of the easiest high-end 3D apps to get to grips with. www.maxon.net

Opposite above: **Softimage|XSI** combines sublime modelling with nonlinear animation, scripting and phenomenal rendering through tight integration with Mental Images' Mental Ray rendering software. It also features an integrated 2D/3D compositor.

Opposite left: **Alias's Maya 3D** software is extremely powerful. Its node-based architecture enables complex animation and rendering linkages to be created and it offers a nonlinear modelling history, plus Mental Ray rendering.
www.alias.com

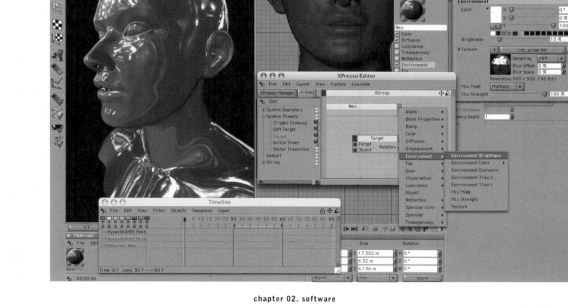

FREE SOFTWARE The latest trend in the high-end 3D market is for the big 3D developers to offer free versions of their packages, slightly modified in some way so that they can't be used commercially. Alias, Softimage and Side Effects Software all produce 'experience' or 'personal learning' versions of their high-end 3D apps. These let you see what it's like to use the latest cutting-edge 3D software for free.

The non-commercial safety features vary from program to program. Alias has the most severe in its version of Maya PLE. The OpenGL shaded display as well as any rendered images are emblazoned with Alias's logo and 'commercial use prohibited by license' just in case you forgot. Maya PLE is not save-disabled but the file format is not compatible with the commercial version of Maya, preventing models being created for free in PLE and opened in Maya commercial. XSI Experience has similar safety measures but they are less intrusive. The best deal is Houdini Apprentice, which has a tiny 'not for commercial use' disclaimer in one corner of the screen and a custom file format.

Below left: **Maya PLE is free to use non-commercially, but has severe watermarking. At least it gives you a taste of what the high-end is all about.**

Below right: **XSI Experience has minimal watermarking and is good for non-commercial use, although rendering size is restricted.**

Demos and personal learning versions are one thing, but what can you get for nothing? Well, surprisingly there are plenty of free 3D programs available. So long as you realize that you're not going to get as slick a package as a commercial 3D app, they are well worth a look.

One of the best free 3D apps available is Blender. This program is a full 3D production package featuring the kinds of tools and functionality you'd expect to see in a mid-range to high-end application. The company that is now developing the program is a non-profit organization, and as such Blender can be downloaded for free from www.blender3d.com. It's available on several platforms, too: Windows, OS X, Linux, Irix, Free BSD and Sun Solaris.

Renderers are also pretty easy to come by, though many of these have been created by computing students and are usually command-line. Some free renderers include Lightflow (www.lightflowtech.com), Virtual Light (www.3dvirtualight.com) and Angle (www.dctsystems.co.uk). POV Ray is a famous free raytrace renderer, but it lacks an easy-to-use GUI.

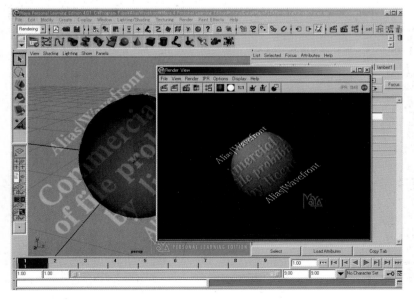

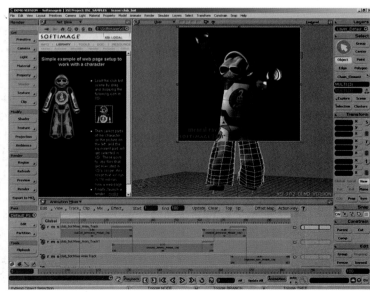

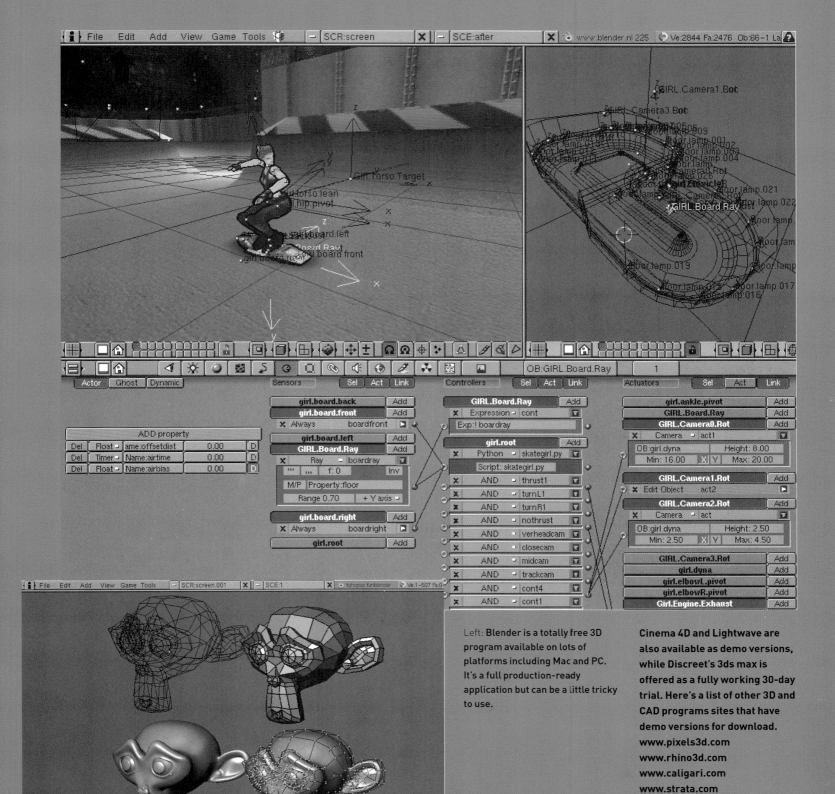

Left: **Blender is a totally free 3D program available on lots of platforms including Mac and PC. It's a full production-ready application but can be a little tricky to use.**

Cinema 4D and Lightwave are also available as demo versions, while Discreet's 3ds max is offered as a fully working 30-day trial. Here's a list of other 3D and CAD programs sites that have demo versions for download.
www.pixels3d.com
www.rhino3d.com
www.caligari.com
www.strata.com
www.autodessys.com
www.eovia.com
www.electricimage.com

CHARACTER GEOMETRY

When it comes to building realistic 3D characters, the topology of the mesh is absolutely crucial if the character is to be animated. For cartoonish characters with rigidly jointed limbs, this is not important since the model will not be animated using deformations; rather each joint will pivot at the joint. For realistic character animation the model usually needs to be built as a single skin (one single net of polygons for the entire body surface).

Single-skin characters have no joints, and the arms, legs, shoulders, etc, are bent using a skeleton of joint deformers inside the model. In order that the mesh deforms correctly, you could simply have the mesh at a massive resolution. However, this would cause all sorts of other problems and would slow down the animation. It's far better to design the mesh properly so that deformations look natural and the model stays light.

Designing proper edge loops is one way to create good character deformation, but you'll probably find it difficult to get a mesh to flow in the way you'd like if you're new to this kind of modelling. One key aspect is to make sure that the model consists of quads only, at least those parts of the mesh that will deform greatly. A quad is simply a four-sided polygon, and this comes with two benefits: first, renderers like quads; and second, quads tend to subdivide better. Most subdivision surface algorithms support triangles and quads, and even N-gons (polygons with more than four sides), but the difference is that Quads seem to subdivide without causing problems. Triangles are okay in some places, not in others, and to be fair, using them is sometimes unavoidable. N-gons, however, are a definite no-no.

When working with a mesh you'll begin to see all the different ways that quads can be connected. Here are some examples you'll come across, and also some special topological devices that will help you when modelling.

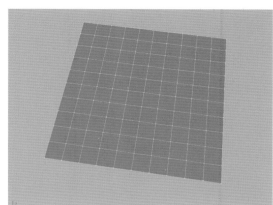

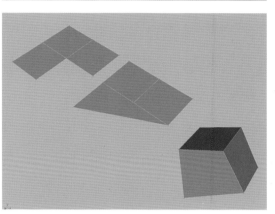

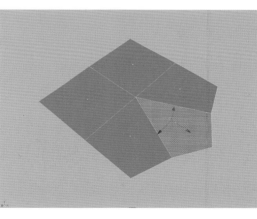

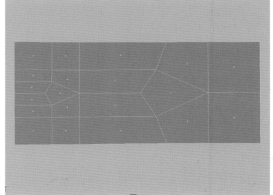

Left, top down: The most common topological pattern for quads is the regular grid. A grid deforms nicely and is topologically very sound. Note that each vertex is connected to four polygons (apart from those at the edges).

Another common topological structure is formed when a vertex is connected to three quads instead of four. This image shows a sequence converting a regular grid of polygons into a junction of three. Take a grid of four quads, delete one, then merge the remaining two vertices. The two groups of polygons on the right are identical, the far right one has been edited into a 3D form to show the junction better. Note that this three-way connection is the same as the corner of a cube and is a useful way to reduce the resolution of the mesh in specific areas or to create branching loops.

The opposite of the three-way junction is where you add rather than remove a polygon to create a vertex that connects to five quads. Count the edges – they are all quads. The selected polygon is one that has been created between the ones either side in this regular grid.

Five-way junctions are very useful for increasing the resolution of a mesh. In this example we begin with only two polygons on the right but as the mesh progresses towards the left, the resolution increases until we have six polygons. Two five-way junctions have been used to produce the increase in resolution while maintaining all-quads in the mesh.

PARTICLE EFFECTS Particles are a special kind of 3D object. With a polygon or NURBS model you want to keep the individual components together in one nicely built object, but with particles you want them to spray out all over the place.

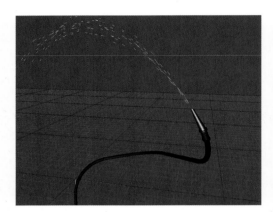

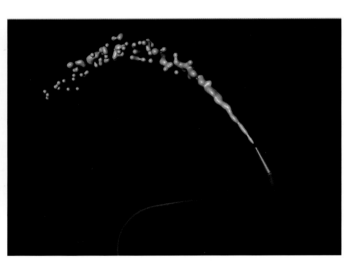

Particles are used for all kinds of effects, particularly in films and television, where they're used to create explosions, smoke, fire, liquids and other volumetric substances.

To create particles you generally start with an emitter – an object that emits particles at a certain rate and direction. A typical emitter would produce a fountain effect where particles are sprayed upwards in a cone, spreading out as they go. If the particles are set to react to gravity, they fall back down once their initial impulse has worn off. You could connect an emitter to the end of a hose object and animate the hose flaying around. The emitter would shoot particles into the scene as it moves, creating the effect of water spraying from the end of the hose.

You don't have to use an emitter to create particles. Objects themselves can be defined as particle emitters. When this is the case, particles are emitted from the surface of the object – either from the vertices or the polygons or randomly. The surface normals are used to define the direction of each particle so that the emission follows the shape of the object.

Far left: **Particles emitted from the end of a hose can be used to simulate a spray of water. However the particles themselves are just points in space. When rendered you won't see any particle effect at all.**

Left above: **In order to create a water effect you need to tell the 3D software what to do. In this case we apply a Metaballs geometry to the particle stream, which generates a blobby surface around each particle point and mingles with surrounding blobs. That's the geometry sorted out, but you still need to texture the object as you would any other.**

Left below: **Applying a custom water material to the blobby object finishes the effect. This water utilizes transparency with refraction, an environmental reflection map and a bump map. The water is animated because of the emitter so a new surface is generated at each frame, creating the illusion of spraying water.**

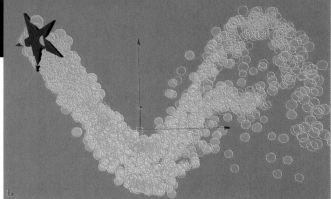

Right: **This star object has been set to emit particles from its surface. As the star moves, the particles fly off in all directions and, when rendered using the appropriate shader settings, creates a glowing shower of sparks that float in its wake.**

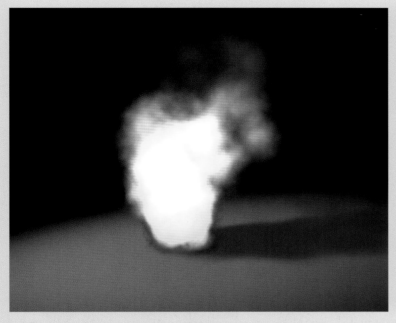

Top left: **Here's a simple volumetric fire and smoke shader attached to a particle emitter. Each particle is rendered as a true volume. The overlapping particles combine to look brighter, and each particle ages over time, becoming less red and bright as it turns to smoke.**

Top right: **A smoke shader is similar except that it's less bright and has no colour. Note that the volumetric object can even cast shadows in the scene.**

Above: **The density of the volume has a great effect over the look of the particle cloud. Some materials, such as dust or snow, can appear dense in certain circumstances. Pyroclastic plumes from a volcano, or avalanches, are good examples. In this case the volume is very thick, and the surface casts and receives shadows. This is key to achieving certain smoke and plume effects.**

WHERE THERE'S SMOKE...

Particles systems are often used to create smoke and fire because there's usually no other way to achieve these effects in 3D. It can be a tricky subject to get right because the movement and texture of smoke or fire is organic and changeable.

One way to accomplish these pyrotechnic effects is to substitute nonrenderable points in the particle system for spheres, which can then be textured to look like fire or smoke. By using a Fresnel shader in the Transparency channel of the material, the edges of the spheres dissolve to nothing, hiding the fact that geometry is being used. This can work well for fire and certain kinds of smoke.

If you want truly realistic smoke plumes, you have to ditch geometry and turn to volumetric rendering techniques. Volumetric rendering calculates the cumulative effect of semi-transparent materials such as smoke and fire by rendering them as a true 3D volume. Whereas a texture map is really just a 2D image, curved and distorted on a 3D surface, a volumetric texture exists in all three dimensions. Rendering such effects can be time-consuming, but the results are worthwhile.

ADVANCED MODELLING – EDGES When modelling practically any rigid (non-organic) object, it is crucial that you model edges correctly. This is something that most beginners in 3D overlook, because it's not obvious at first. But if you wonder why your 3D work just doesn't seem to look truly professional, this could be the reason.

If you look round your room or office, you'll see many real objects that have corners and edges. A table has a flat top with perpendicular sides that meet at 90°, and a CD case likewise. To take a slightly more complex example, look at the end of a ballpoint pen, with a domed cap stoppering a hexagonal shaft – all have edges.

You may be able to visualize simple 3D shapes that can easily represent these objects: a cube for the table top, an extruded profile for the CD case or a cropped sphere and a cylinder for the pen. The problem is that in our quest to break down the real objects mentally into essential forms, it's too easy to oversimplify them, and the edges are often the first things to go.

Left: **Here's the end of a pen, modelled using our deconstruction technique. All the parts are basically correct but the object looks fake. The reason is that all the edges are too sharp. In fact, the edges are perfect – something that never happens in reality.**

Below: **Here's the same object modelled more accurately. First we create a hexagon spline, then we round off the edges by chamfering the points.**

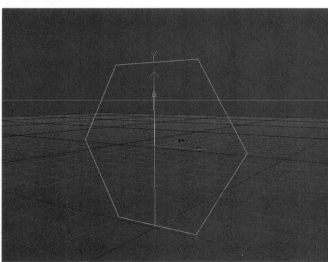

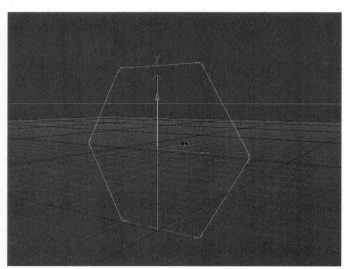

Below: These are lofted together with some circles to create the shaft of the pen. The end of a ballpoint pen has a non-hexagonal section, recreated here. The chamfered hexagons produce a softer, rounded edge to the edges of the pen, reflecting the original.

Bottom left: The cap of the loft is rounded. In the program we're using here, Cinema 4D, the rounding can be achieved parametrically; it's built into the Loft feature, so we just need to enable it and set the radius and subdivision. Already the object looks more solid and realistic.

Below: The cap is made not with a sphere but a lathe. The profile of the cap is not domed, it's angled – again, chamfering of the vertices helps to prevent any perfectly hard edges. Note that the underside is also chamfered so that the cap does not intersect the top of the shaft. The intersection would be another perfect edge.

Bottom right: The pen is rerendered in the same scene, and the results are remarkably better. Using an ordinary object like this is a good way to demonstrate the effect of edge detail in an object, because there is nothing else in the scene to support the realism of the model.

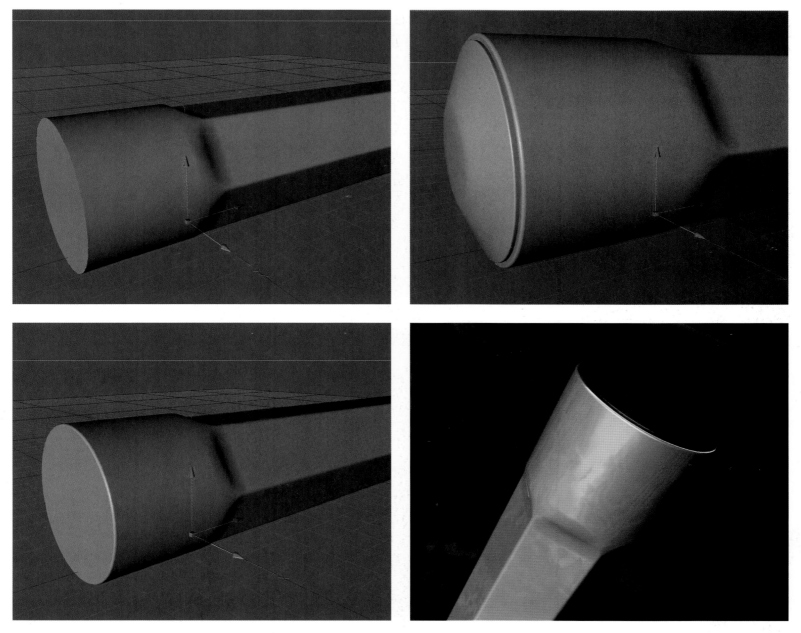

LOGO AND TYPE Type and logos are excellent subjects for 3D treatment and have been so since 3D began. The principle is extremely simple: take a logo, or some text, and extrude it to give it depth. This produces type that extends into the 3D dimension and can be treated like any other 3D object.

When creating 3D type there's one crucial thing to remember, and that's the edges of the text. When type is set in 2D on a page there's no problem with its readability (so long as the font is meant to be readable). We read text by recognizing the edges of the letters and the overall shape of the word, so black text on a white background is easy to read. Take text into a 3D program and extrude it and you complicate the edges of the text, especially if you choose a dramatic camera angle.

Above: **Black text on a white page is easy to read. You can see the letter shapes easily and you can readily recognize the shapes of the words. For brand logos it's important for the type or artwork to be easily recognizable.**

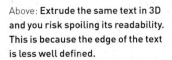

Above: **Extrude the same text in 3D and you risk spoiling its readability. This is because the edge of the text is less well defined.**

Right: **A simple way to check readability is to view the alpha mask of the text object. As you can see, it's not clear what word this is supposed to be.**

Above left: **There are a few reasons why the 3D type is not reading well. There is not very much contrast between the front face of the type and the extruded side. This is partly to do with the lighting. A quick adjustment of the lighting increases the contrast between the sides and the face making the type a little easier to recognize.**

Above right: **It's still pretty confusing, so let's change the camera angle to make the type less distorted. Head-on and slightly from below keeps the type readable and also shows off the 3D-ness nicely. The depth of the type doesn't need to be overstated for it to look good in a still image.**

Right: **Another technique for improving the readability of 3D type is to have different colours for the face and sides of the type. Most 3D programs let you do this, although you can also do it manually by selecting the face polygons and creating a new object from them. As an alternative, you could use coloured lights.**

LIGHTING AND ILLUMINATION Lighting is crucial to any 3D scene, whether photorealistic or not. Lighting conveys mood and time of day and illuminates the form of objects in the scene. A poorly lit scene will never look convincing, no matter how great the animation, modelling or texturing.

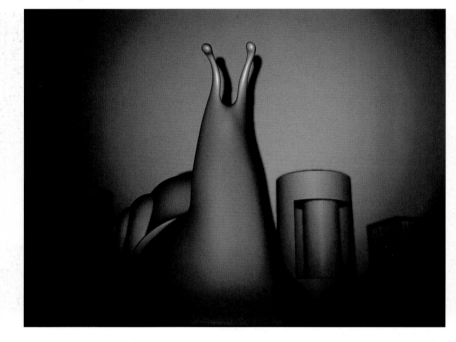

Lights have a few basic properties, and it will help to recognize and evaluate these independently of one another if you want to translate what you see in reality to the computer. These properties are intensity, colour, spread and direction. You can look at any photograph and evaluate the lighting using these terms.

To take a simple example, imagine a shot of a beach at high noon, midsummer on a cloudless day. Now think about the scene in terms of the properties above. Intensity: very high direct illumination from the sun results

Above left: **Here's a poor example of lighting. One spotlight illuminates the scene, and it's placed in line with the camera so that the light is head-on. This flattens out the renders, foreshortening the scene, and making object details difficult to see.**

Above right: **By moving the light up and to the side, we get much more spatial information in the scene. The Snail is brought forward in the image, and the depth of the scene is enhanced. But shadows are quite dark.**

in high contrast with bright highlights; the bright light also results in a high amount of bounced light which makes some shadow area less dense. Colour: white with subtle blue ambient light from the skydome. Spread: with the sun, there is no attenuation of the light. Direction: depending on the location, from almost directly above.

Now imagine a street scene at night. It's raining. Intensity: very low, but with bright areas from artificial street lighting, and maybe some slight ambience from reflected light from low clouds and dark shadows. Colour: A murky monotone orange. Spread: streetlights are strongly attenuated over distance and are throwing limited cones of light into the scene. Direction: straight down from the streetlights.

Left: A dim blue fill light on the opposite side of the scene fills in the shadow areas, providing some extra detail without washing the image out.

Below left: The previous two lights are reduced in intensity to about 10 per cent each and both aimed at the background objects only. The foreground subject is then illuminated with its own spotlight directly above. This not only picks out the subject more clearly but add a strong sense of isolation to the character in the scene.

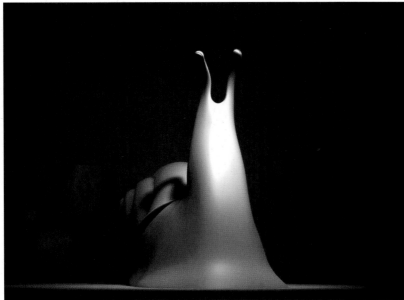

Above: Another version of the same scene makes use of extra fill lighting on the snail and depth-of-field blurring for a more cinematic look and a forlorn feel for the central character.

Left: Lighting the background brightly and reducing the illumination of the subject turns the character into a silhouette. The result still focuses attention on the subject but in a more introverted, subtle way.

NEGATIVE LIGHTS AND FALLOFF Lights in a 3D program can be set to cast negative illumination. This feature, available in most 3D programs, causes light not to be cast into the scene but to be sucked out of it. There is no real-world counterpart to this effect, of course, which is a useful byproduct of the 3D graphics systems.

Below: **Here are three spotlights with different falloff so you can see the effect. The left light has no falloff, the middle light has linear falloff, and the right light has inverse squared falloff. You can usually set different degrees of falloff, depending on the amount of attenuation required.**

3D lights can be set so that they decay naturally, preventing their illumination spilling too far into the scene. This is a very useful feature, as it allows you some control over the lighting spread, helping to restrict it to where it is needed. Light falloff mimics the inverse-square law that governs the decay of light in the real world.

Opposite top left: **Falloff only goes so far. To mop up overspill from a light in specific places, you need negative lights. Take this example – one object casting a shadow over another. The green cylinder appears to be floating because there's nothing tying it visually to the floor on which it rests; it's already in shadow and the ambient and fill lights also used in the scene do not cast shadows.**

Opposite top right: **A negative light with a short falloff is placed under the cylinder to darken the floor under it. This makes it look as if there's also some subtle ambient shadowing, as if the scene had been rendered using radiosity.**

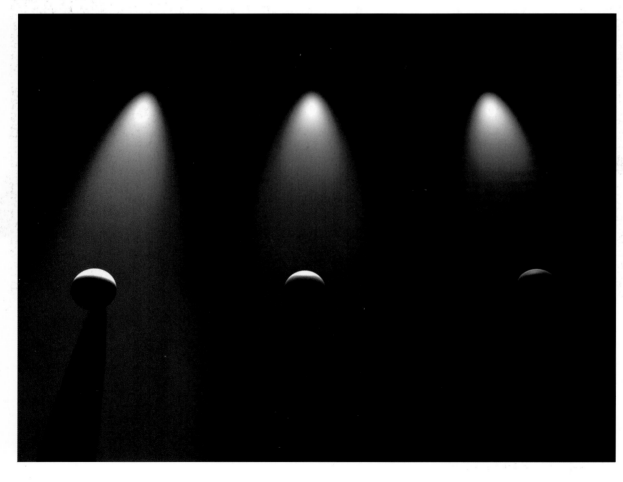

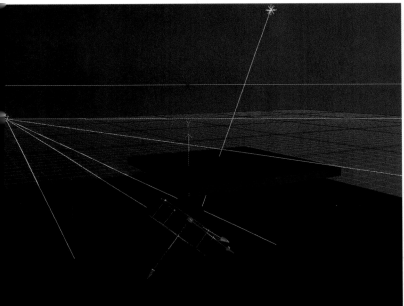

Above: **Here's the scene in shaded view in Cinema 4D. You can see the three positive lights used in the scene (parallel, point fill and ambient) plus the negative light at the base of the cylinder. In Cinema 4D, unlike some other apps, there is a special parallel spotlight that gives a disk-like shadow. A very short falloff distance is used, along with a low brightness.**

Above: **Negative lights can also be used for special effects. Whereas positive lights cast dark shadows, negative lights cast bright ones. In this example, two shadow-casting point lights, one positive and one negative, and a blur fill, illuminate the subject. The positive light casts** a normal dark shadow but the negative light is casting a light shadow. Uses of negative lights aren't always obvious, but it can be helpful to experiment with these effects, especially in illustration and creative design.

MATERIALS AND SURFACES The ability to simulate an object accurately in 3D has a lot to do with the surface quality of the object when it is rendered. Texture maps, material settings and procedural shaders all combine to create a believable representation of a real or imagined object.

Designing surfaces is an art in itself, but one that can be mastered with practice and perseverance. Just as with modelling or lighting, you need to break down an object's appearance into components to evaluate and then replicate it in 3D. With 3D surfaces it's that much easier because a 3D program's material system is usually structured in a compartmentalized way. In reality most of the surface properties of an object are the result of a single phenomena – the reflection of light off its surface – but a 3D program breaks them down into specific components: Diffuse, Specular, Ambient (or, correctly, Luminosity), reflection, transparency and bump. Some 3D programs have even more components, such as translucence, or split the components mentioned above into further subcomponents (such as Diffuse into colour and diffusion).

Ambient   Reflection   Bump   Specular   Diffuse

Above: **Here's a real object that displays most of the typical surface components.** Specular highlights are really reflections, and you can just make out some detail here of a window (the highlight is slightly square). Diffuse is the general illumination of the object surface, brightest facing the light and dimmer in areas not in direct line of sight of the main light source.

Ambient/Luminosity is the darkest part of the surface, and in this case it's very dark because, like most objects, the vase isn't self-illuminating. Glowing objects would have a high Ambient/Luminosity setting. The bump property shows all over the surface in various dimples, nicks and scratches.

Right: Here's the 3D version of the same object. We've used several texture maps created in Photoshop, as well as a digital photo for the flower fabric, to recreate the object. The scene is rendered using radiosity so that the lighting matches the photo reference a little better. It's by no means perfect – a quick sketch rather than the finished work – but it shows you how much detail is required for even a simple surface like this vase.

Below: This is the diffuse/colour texture used on the vase. It's loaded into the Color channel in Cinema 4D but it controls both the diffuse brightness and the colour.

Below left: The bump map is also created in Photoshop. It has some large-scale clumping, which is quite low in contrast. This helps to create large-scale undulations in the surface. Finer 'blips' create depressions in the surface, and these are darker and more intense because we want their bumps to be stronger.

Below: Reflection is enabled and a Fresnel shader is applied to attenuate the reflection on those parts of the surface that will be viewed head-on.

Left: Creating realistic humans is one of the most difficult jobs in 3D. Creating them with believable character and photoreal surfacing and lighting is nearly impossible. The quality of Koji Yamagami's stunning 3D render almost defies belief. But it's no surprise. Using 3DS Max and Splutterfish's Brazil rendering plug-in, Koji routinely creates images like this for his company Beans Magic Co.
Koji Yamagami
www.beans-magic.com/

Below:The still life reinterpreted by the Valencian 3D artist Carles Piles. Piles models and textures in Maxon Cinema 4D, then applies an intensive spot-lighting regime to balance realism against his trademark painterly style. He then readjusts the shading for an optimal effect. "My goal is just one; to imagine something, obtain sufficient visual references for what I imagined, and then create it."
Carles Piles
www.carlespiles.com

Below: It's rare to find a 3D artist who can bend, mould and soften 3D imagery into something much more organic and natural, and Francois Gutherz is one of the those rarities. Combining a 3D renderer with Photoshop is a good way to create less sterile-looking 3D work, of which Francois is a prime exponent.
Francois Gutherz
www.fra.planet-d.net

Right: There are few 3D artists whose work is so immediately recognizable (or disturbing) as Meats Meier. While currently employed at The Orphanage, a special-effects house in San Francisco, Meats still finds time to create personal works of art and work on freelance projects. "My goal is to one day be the first person to complete a full-length 3D movie completely on my own. To reach this goal I have spent the last seven years studying every needed skill—modelling, texturing, rigging, animation, lighting, rendering and everything from compositing to sound editing."

Above: Meats says, "My artwork is as close to free-flow creation as is possible, after years of hardcore practice most things are finally second nature. The power of 3D art is that you can build one sculpture and by positioning it differently, changing the lighting and camera angles, you can have a new image. To do this with traditional paint would be impossible."

Opposite: "With 3D," Meats adds, "the possibilities are 'virtually' endless. I usually end up with at least 200 images before I get bored with a concept. I enjoy looking back and being able to see what led up to what I would call a final image. Also, I can see other paths that I could have chosen along the way, which usually leads to the next concept..."
Meats Meier
www.3dartspace.com

MEATS MEIER

Below: Carles Piles' lizard is a brilliant example of how modelling and texturing can work together to create great images. The balance between what is geometry and what is a bump map is perfect.
Carles Piles
www.carlespiles.com

Left: Architectural 3D artist Chen Qingfeng's work combines great modelling with even better lighting and rendering, an essential skill for architectural 3D work. Chen's images are rendered using radiosity techniques with Autodesk's Lightscape.
Chen Qingfeng
cqfcqf.digitalart.org

Left: Moving and modelling one head and four limbs is hard enough, but Daniel Phillips pushes the boundaries by creating a character with three heads and six limbs on a single torso. We can only imagine how tricky it would be to rig and animate this monstrous character.
Daniel Phillips
http://dcp.lihp.com

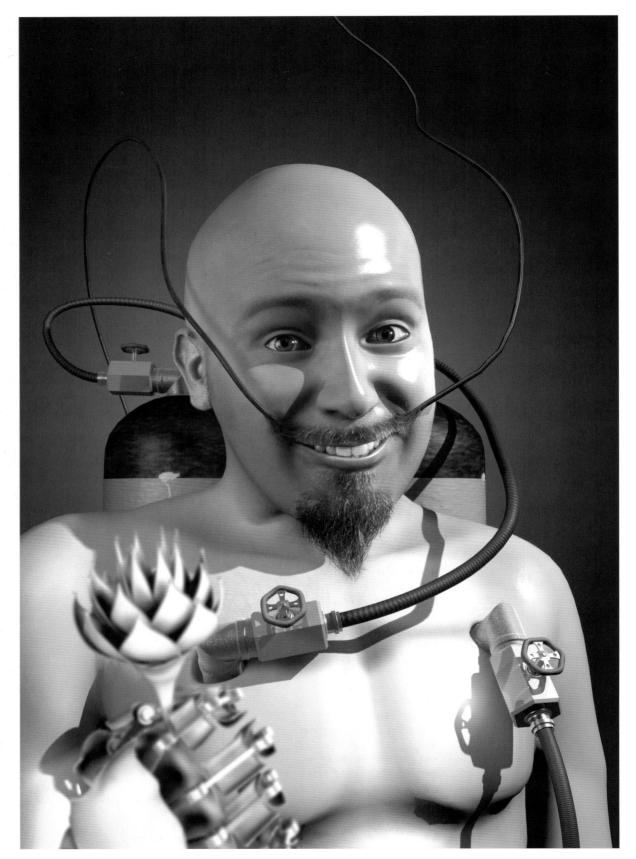

Right: **Peder Aversten's 3D work is humorous, quirky, and cool. This image was created by building 3D models in Maya and then overlaying them with still images in Photoshop.** "Art is a way of living for me. I do fine-art, sculpture, digital art, 3D and video production. You could almost classify it as multimedia because I like to experiment a lot."
Peder Aversten
aversten@meshmen.com

Above: Combine intense model making with photoreal surfacing, lighting and rendering and you get the wonderful work of Reinhard Claus. The details in this teapot model have been constructed with an intense eye for detail, and this goes double for the surface material. An HDRI environment adds the necessary reflections and highlights in this excellent render.
Reinhard Claus
rc@claus-figuren.de

Right: **US-born, Berlin-based David Maas produced this 3D illustration for German power company EAM.** David is an illustrator and 3D artist using Lightwave, and says of the image he created, "In the original street poster, one penguin is showing off his new pad and bragging about the cheap cooling costs: 'it wasn't cheap but the living costs are a joke.' It was so popular that the agency commissioned an encore: these two blokes ended up illustrating an entire brochure. The 3D approach made it economical, as the same figures and objects could be reused in new poses."
David Maas
www.stickman.de

REFERENCE

GLOSSARY

Aliasing The jagged edge of bitmapped images or fonts occurring either when aliasing resolution is insufficient or when the images have been enlarged. This is caused by the pixels – which are square with straight sides – making up the image becoming visible. Sometimes called 'jaggies', 'staircasing' or 'stairstepping.'

Alpha channel A place where information regarding the transparency of a pixel is kept. In image files this is a separate channel – additional to the three RGB channels – where 'masks' are stored.

Ambient A term used in 3D modelling software to describe a light source with no focus or direction, such as that which results from bouncing off all objects in a scene.

Antialiasing A technique of optically eliminating the jagged effect of bitmapped images or text reproduced on low-resolution devices such as monitors. This is achieved by blending the colour at the edges of the object with its background by averaging the density of the range of pixels involved. Antialiasing is also employed to filter texture maps, such as those used in 3D applications, to eliminate signs of pixelation.

API (Application Programming Interface) A layer of code, built in or added to a computer operating system, which creates a bridge between an application (e.g. a 3D package) and computer hardware (e.g. a 3D graphics card). As long as both the software and the hardware support the same API, neither needs to be configured to support the other, enabling many applications to run on many different types of hardware without any need for recoding.

Area light A special light type that emits from a 2D area rather than a single point.

Axis An imaginary line that defines the centre of the 3D universe. In turn, the x, y and z axes (width, height and depth, respectively) define each of the three dimensions of an object. The axis along which an object rotates is the axis of rotation.

B-Spline A type of curve, similar to a Bezier curve but based on more complex formulae. B-Splines have additional control points and values, allowing a higher degree of control over a more localized area.

Bevel To round or chamfer an edge. Can also mean to extrude a polygon along its Normal, producing bevels around its perimeter.

Bézier spline In 3D and drawing applications, a curved line between two 'control' points. Each point is a tiny database, or 'vector', storing data about the line, such as its thickness, colour, length and direction. Complex shapes can be applied to the curve by manipulating 'handles', which are dragged out from the control points.

Blend The merging of two or more colours, forming a gradual transition from one to the other.

Boolean Named after G. Boole, a 19th-century English mathematician, Boolean is used to describe a shorthand for logical computer operations, such as those that link values ('and', 'or', 'not', 'nor', etc., called 'Boolean operators'). In 3D applications, these operations can be used to join two objects together or remove one shape from another.

Bounding Box A rectangular box, available in certain applications, which encloses an item so that it can be resized or moved. In 3D applications, the bounding box is parallel to the axes of the object.

Bump map A bitmap image file, normally grayscale, applied to a surface material. The gray values in the image are assigned height values, with black representing the troughs and white the peaks. When applied to a surface and rendered the surface takes on an impression of relief.

CAD (computer-aided design) Strictly speaking, any design carried out using a computer, but the term is generally used with reference to 3D design, such as product design or architecture, where a computer software application is used to construct and develop complex structures.

Camera A viewpoint in a 3D application, defined by position, angle and lens properties, used to generate a view of a scene during modelling or rendering. Cameras can also be moved during animation, in the same way a movie camera moves during a conventional shoot.

Cartesian coordinates The coordinate system employed in 3D applications, which uses numbers to locate points in 3D space in relation to a theoretical point of origin where the three dimensional axes intersect.

Channel A bitmap image or a set of parameters used to define a component of a texture material.

Clipping plane In 3D applications, a plane beyond which an object is not visible. Most 3D views have six clipping planes: top, bottom, left, right, front and back.

Collision detection The ability of a 3D program to calculate the proximity of objects and prevent them from intersecting.

Concave polygon A polygon whose shape is concave, for example, a star shape.

Convex polygon A polygon whose shape is convex, for example, a regular hexagon shape.

Coordinates Numerical values that define locations in 2D or 3D space.

Diffuse A colour texture map applied to a surface to define its colours when viewed in direct light, and how much of the light that hits that surface will be absorbed and how much will be reflected – i.e. how much of that colour we can see.

part 07. reference

Digital Anything operated by, or created from, information or signals represented by binary digits, such as a digital recording. As distinct from analogue, in which information is represented by a physical variable (in a recording this may be via the grooves in a vinyl platter).

Displacement map A grayscale bitmap image which operates similarly to a bump map, but differs in that the black, white and grey values will affect the geometry of the surface underneath. Displacement mapping creates a more realistic texture than bump mapping at the cost of additional time computing the effects.

Environment map A 2D image that is projected onto the surface of a 3D object to simulate an environmental reflection.

Extrapolate Creating new values for a parameter based on the values that have gone before.

Extrude The process of duplicating the cross section of a 2D object, placing it in a 3D space at a distance from the original and creating a surface that joins the two together. For example, when extruded, two circles become a tube.

Face In 3D modelling, one flat 'side' of an object, e.g. one of six sides of a cube.

Fall-off In a 3D environment, the degree to which light or another parameter loses intensity away from its source.

Fillet A curved surface that is created between two adjoining or intersecting surfaces. Fillets turn up most frequently in NURBS modelling.

Forward Kinematics Traditional animation is based on Forward Kinematics, where, for example, to make a character reach for an object, first the upper arm is rotated, then the forearm and then the hand.

Frame An individual still image extracted from an animation sequence. The basic divisor of time in animation.

Fresnel An effect where the edge of an object brightens due to an increased intensity of reflection along the edge.

Function curve In an application, a user-definable curve used to control the speed or intensity of motion or an effect.

Geometry What 3D objects are made out of, or rather described by. Geometry types include polygons, NURBS and Bézier patches.

Gimbal lock In 3D applications, a situation in which an object cannot be rotated around one or more axes.

Glow A material parameter used to create external glows on objects. The glow usually extends beyond the object surface by a defined amount.

Height map An image used to displace or deform geometry. See Displacement Map.

Hidden Surface Removal A rendering method, usually wireframe, that prevents surfaces that cannot be seen from the given view from being drawn.

Interpolation A computer calculation used to estimate unknown values that fall between known ones. One use of this process is to redefine pixels in bitmapped images after they have been modified in some way – for instance, when an image is resized (called 'resampling') or rotated, or if colour corrections have been made. In such cases the program makes estimates from the known values of other pixels lying in the same or similar ranges.

Inverse Kinematics Or IK for short. When animating hierarchical models, IK can be applied so that moving the lowest object in the hierarchy has an effect on all the objects further up. This is the inverse of how Forward Kinematics works.

Lathe In 3D applications, the technique of creating a 3D object by rotating a 2D profile around an axis – just like carving a piece of wood on a real lathe.

Layer Modern image-editing applications can separate elements of an image onto transparent layers, stacked on top of each other to form a composite image. By switching layers on and off, changing their order, or changing the way they interact with each other, a designer can rework the composite image in a vast number of ways.

Map An image applied to a texture channel of a material.

Material The aggregate of all surface attributes for an object.

Memory The recall of digital data on a computer. Typically, this refers to either 'dynamic RAM', the volatile 'random access' memory that is emptied when a computer is switched off (data need to be stored on media such as a hard disk for future renewal), or ROM, the stable 'read only' memory that contains unchanging data, for example the basic startup and initialization functions of most computers.

Mesh Vertices Vertices that are linked together to form Polygon or NURBS (or other) surfaces.

Motion channel An animation parameter that controls how an object moves (for example, rotation x, y, z and translation x, y, z are all Motion channels).

Multi-pass rendering The process whereby a single scene is rendered in multiple passes, each pass producing an image (or movie or image sequence) containing a specific portion of the scene but not all of it (for example, one part of a multi-pass render may contain just the reflections in the scene, or just the specular highlights).

Normal In 3D objects, the direction that is perpendicular to the surface of the polygon to which it relates.

NURBS Non-Uniform Rational B-Spline. A B-spline curve or a mesh of B-spline curves used to

GLOSSARY

define a line or a surface in a 3D application. NURBs surfaces require fewer points than polygons to model smooth flowing surfaces.

Parallax The apparent movement of two objects relative to each other when viewed from different positions.

Phong shading A superior method of shading surfaces that computes the shading of every pixel by interpolating data from the surface normals.

Pixel Acronym of picture element. The smallest component of a digitally generated image, such as a single dot of light on a computer monitor.

Plug-in A small program that 'plugs-in' to an application to extend its features or add support for a particular file format.

Polygon Any 2D shape with more than three sides. Polygons – usually triangles, but sometimes quads – are joined together in 3D applications to create the surfaces of 3D objects.

Primitive A basic geometric element (e.g. a cylinder, pyramid or cube) from which more complex objects can be built.

Quad A four-point polygon.

Raycasting A simplified form of raytracing, where the effects of direct light on a model is traced by the rendering engine, but not the effects of light bouncing off or between surfaces.

Raytracing A rendering algorithm that simulates the physical and optical properties

of light rays as they reflect off a 3D model, producing realistic shadows and reflections.

Real-time An operation where the computer calculates and displays the results as the user watches. Real-time rendering, for example, enables the user to move around a 3D scene or remodel objects on the screen without having to wait for the display to update.

Refraction The effect where rays of light are bent, typically when passing through one medium to another, such as air to water.

Rendering The process of creating a 2D image from 3D geometry to which lighting effects and surface textures have been applied.

Scale A 3D transformation that shrinks or enlarges an object about one or more axes.

Shading The process of filling in the polygons of a 3D model with respect to viewing angle and lighting conditions so that it resembles a solid object.

Skin In 3D applications, a surface stretched over a series of 'ribs', such as an aircraft wing.

Specular map In 3D applications, a texture map – such as those created by noise filters – that is used instead of specular colour to control highlights.

Stitching A technique in NURBS modelling whereby two or more surfaces are joined along their boundaries.

Surface In 3D applications, the matrix of control points and line end points underlying a mapped texture or colour.

Sweep The process of creating a 3D object by moving a 2D profile along a path.

Texture The surface definition of an object.

Triangle The simplest type of polygon, made from three connected vertices.

UV coordinates In a 3D environment, a system of rectangular 2D coordinates used to apply a texture map to a 3D surface.

Vertex Another name for a point (polygons) or control point (NURBS).

View A window in a 3D program depicting the 3D scene from a given vantage.

Wireframe A skeletal view of a computer-generated 3D object before the surface rendering has been applied.

Z-Buffer A 3D renderer that solves the problem of rendering two pixels in the same place (one in front of the other) by calculating and storing the distance of each pixel from the camera (the 'z-distance'), then rendering the nearest pixel last.

INDEX